Managing to survi

Asylum seekers, refugees and access to social housing

Roger Zetter and Martyn Pearl

The
Housing
Associations
Charitable
Trust

The POLICY
P~P
PRESS

THE HOUSING
CORPORATION

First published in Great Britain in 1999 by

The Policy Press
University of Bristol
34 Tyndall's Park Road
Bristol BS8 1PY
UK

Tel   +44 (0)117 954 6800
Fax   +44 (0)117 973 7308
E-mail tpp@bristol.ac.uk
http://www.bristol.ac.uk/Publications/TPP

ISBN 1 86134 171 7

Roger Zetter is Professor and Deputy Head and **Martyn Pearl** is Principal Lecturer and Director of the Housing Studies Unit, both at the School of Planning, Oxford Brookes University.

Cover design by Qube Design Associates, Bristol.
Printed in Great Britain by Hobbs the Printers Ltd, Southampton.

Contents

Acknowledgements

The authors acknowledge the significant part played by both Dr Azim El-Hassan and David Griffiths in the production of the manuscript for this report. Both brought their considerable knowledge and skill to the project and undertook much of the fieldwork on which this report is based. Without them, the work would have been significantly diminished. Thanks also to Sarah Birtles who provided welcome advice and support to get the project up and running.

We are also grateful to The Housing Corporation, in particular Adrian Moran and Barbara Carlisle, for their funding and continued support, and to HACT, and Reena Mukherji for advice, support and additional, top-up funding. Both organisations were also represented on the project steering group, which also comprised David Ashmore, Chinta Kallie and Areti Sianni. We are grateful for their time and expertise.

Finally, we would like to thank those individuals and organisations prepared to offer time and information to our study. Without their input this study would not have been possible.

Glossary of terms

ALG	Association of London Government
ARHAG	African Refugee Housing Association
AWHA	Arawak/Walton Housing Association
BME	Black and Minority Ethnic (RSLs)
CORE	Continuous Recording (of data) by The Housing Corporation
ECHA	English Churches Housing Association
EFHA	Ealing Family Housing Association
ELR	Exceptional Leave to Remain
ETHG	East Thames Housing Group
FBHO	Federation of Black Housing Organisations
HACT	Housing Associations Charitable Trust
HMO	Houses in Multiple Occupation
IGP	Innovation and Good Practice Grant
ILR	Indefinite Leave to Remain
LBGU	London Boroughs Grants Unit
MHT	Metropolitan Housing Trust
NHHT	Notting Hill Housing Trust

OCHA	Oxford Citizens Housing Association
PRHA	Providence Row Housing Association
RAGDS	Rent-in-Advance Guarantee/Deposit Schemes
RAP	Refugee Arrivals Project
RCO	Refugee Community-based Organisation
RHA	Refugee Housing Association
RNAC	Refugee and New Arrivals Coordinator
RSL	Registered Social Landlord
SHA	Springboard Housing Association
SHG	Social Housing Grant
SHMG	Supported Housing Management Grant
SMHA	St Mungo's Housing Association
SNMA	Special Need Management Allowance
SSD	Social Services Department
TRAG	Tamil Refugee Action Group (now TRHA)
TSNMA	Transitional Special Needs Management Allowance
WHA	Wandle Housing Association

Introduction

Aims and objectives

Housing provision for refugees and asylum seekers by Registered Social Landlords (RSLs) in England has expanded considerably in the last two to three years. This is the outcome of fundamental changes in government policy introduced through statutes in 1993 and 1996. This report reviews the impact of these changes and the future implications for RSLs. But this is set within a much wider context of housing provision and support services.

This report is the result of an in-depth study, mainly funded by an Innovation and Good Practice Grant (IGP) from The Housing Corporation, with additional financial support from the Housing Associations Charitable Trust (HACT). The study is intended to assist practitioners working or associated with housing provision for refugees and/or asylum seekers. It provides information about the needs of this group and the context of their housing needs; documents existing good practice; and recommends ways in which this practice might be developed further in partnership with the needs and aspirations of consumers.

The quality of RSL service provision and the range of management practices and support are assessed from the point of view of both the providers themselves, and from the perspective of the beneficiaries – the refugees and asylum seekers. By relating their experiences to those of the providers, we aim to shed light on the challenges, successes and barriers to the delivery of good practice in housing supply by the RSLs.

Although the focus of the study is on RSLs and good practice, inevitably the scope is much wider. Because of the continuing upheaval and uncertainty which surrounds provision for this client group, the evaluation is set within a broader framework of policy analysis (see also Marsh and Sangster, 1998). To this extent the study is, in effect, the first nationally based assessment of how the major policy changes, introduced between 1993 and 1996, have affected housing supply processes for this client group.

The aims of the study are:

- to examine the experience of RSLs in providing housing for refugees and asylum seekers;
- to examine the responses of RSLs to the measures contained in the *1996 Asylum and Immigration Act*; and
- to document from this experience, what is sustainable and good practice.

Much of the data and information have been collected through detailed case studies in London, Manchester and Birmingham, and our sources have included policy makers, practitioners and service users. Our aim has been to provide a balanced picture of the current situation facing refugees and asylum seekers (or *persons from abroad* as they are referred to in the legislation) seeking accommodation in the UK. The intention has been to illustrate the diversity of approach in these different locations, but also to gauge the comparability of the London experience with that of other large cities.

Most of the study was completed before the government's proposals for the review of policy for asylum seekers, announced in the July 1998 White Paper and the Bill, *Fairer, faster and firmer: A modern approach to immigration and asylum* (Home Office, 1998) and, subsequently, the *1999 Asylum and Immigration Bill*. But because of the importance of the government's White Paper and the Bill, and because many of our findings directly relate to some of its key proposals, we have incorporated responses to it in this report (Chapter 7). The proposals in the White Paper, which the government is implementing with its legislation in 1999, will heighten the urgent need to address many of the recommendations and measures for improving practice identified in this report.

Orienting the study

Our approach to the study

Research on refugees and asylum seekers is challenging. The subject area is politically sensitive. The study population is difficult to access. Refugees and asylum seekers are understandably sensitive to perceptions, images and misinformation about them; their situation generates few supporters outside those actively involved in advocating their case. Nevertheless, the population constitutes a relatively small but distinctive social group in the UK which, although quite widely dispersed nationally, tends to be clustered in urban areas.

Housing is a key resource in the resettlement of asylum seekers and refugees themselves. The security, shelter and personal space which housing provides are vital elements in the process of regaining the dignity and independence often denied to them through persecution, incarceration and torture in their countries of origin. Hence the significance of the study.

From the point of view of service providers, such as RSLs, the lack of reliable, detailed data, and limited research about the resettlement needs and experiences of refugees and asylum seekers, are barriers to identifying good practice. The crisis created by the current battery of statutory, judicial and policy constraints highlights the need for more

detailed knowledge about this client group. It is this lack of knowledge, particularly with regard to the responses of RSLs, which this report aims to overcome.

The need for the study arises because asylum seekers, and the organisations providing them with care and support, have found the policy 'goal posts' prone to alarming movement in recent years. This uncertainty has often left those in desperate need of help unsure where it might best be obtained and it has created considerable obstacles for those attempting to provide housing and support. This ambiguity has been created in part by government legislation and its accompanying policy machinery. But the invidious position endured by refugees and asylum seekers reflects more fundamentally the policies of restrictionism and competition for public assistance from already massively over-burdened resources. Despite the sympathies for individuals and their households seeking asylum, for national and local government the commitment they represent often generates an unwelcome call on resources.

The diversity and unpredictability of people seeking asylum militates against the production of a comprehensive manual of refugee and asylum seeker practice. The random nature of human conflict, political uncertainty and environment disaster will continue to create unexpected refugees out of apparently settled communities. The groups and organisations examined here cannot, therefore, represent more than an illustrative sample of the communities touched by the process.

Scale of demand

It is impossible to provide an accurate estimate of how many refugees and asylum seekers currently reside in the UK and how this impacts on housing demand. This is partly due to the fact that those with full refugee status are absorbed into aggregate social data; they are not accounted for separately. Census data do not indicate the numbers or distribution of refugee households. Access to Immigration and Nationality Department data is impossible. The only obvious source of data tends to be rather sketchy, anecdotal knowledge of past practice, or partial surveys of particular groups of refugees and asylum seekers or particular location specific studies. A further reason for the lack of data is that few housing organisations record refugees as a distinct category, and, moreover, perceive apparently little recognition of the need to do so. Nor has such information been recorded by RSLs through the CORE (Continuous Recording) returns. Thus, from the point of view of the providers of social housing provision and support services for refugees and asylum seekers, it is difficult to assess accurately the extent of RSL involvement.

For asylum seekers, the problems of statistical analysis are slightly different. The available data represent only a partial picture. Many asylum seekers are reluctant to declare themselves, especially if their applications have been refused. As a result, many simply 'disappear' and therefore go unrecorded.

Data are available from government statistics, but these do not indicate the nature or distribution of housing demand. Overall, between 1985 and 1996, 67,000 heads of households were permitted to stay, of which 12,000 were granted full refugee status. Roughly 20% of applicants receive full refugee status. As a result of the main changes in legislation *(1993 Asylum and Immigration Appeals Act, 1996 Asylum and Immigration Act, 1996 Housing Act,* discussed below and mainly in Appendix A), asylum applications dropped from 44,000 in 1995 to 29,600 in 1996 (Home Office, 1998). In that year nearly 49,000 decisions were reached, over 38,000 applicants were rejected – an increase of nearly 50% on the previous year – and only just over 2,200 accorded full refugee status which is consistent with the previous year (UNHCR, 1997). Some 52,000 cases and 21,000 appeals were pending in mid-1998 at the time of the government's proposals for policy review (Home Office, 1998); by September there were 57,500 cases pending. As of October 1997, the average length of time for determinations ranged from 13.8 months for post-*1993 Asylum and Immigration Appeals Act* applications, up to 58.2 months for pre-1993 applications. When decisions are finally made, of the 29,880 outcomes during 1997, 76% were refusals. The refusal rate in 1998 was about 65%. Applications for asylum rose in 1998 with an average 3,500 per month.

As an indication of the current crisis in housing provision, in mid-May 1998, the London boroughs supported 9,358 adults, 5,387 families with children and 855 unaccompanied children (ALG, 1998). These numbers are increasing. It is certainly the case that demand is largely concentrated in conurbations. It is greatest in London, and to a lesser extent in the rest of southern Britain. Social housing is in short supply and asylum seekers have found access extremely difficult. Moreover, issues of access are not solely related to eligibility of households, but also the availability of suitable housing. Despite assumptions to the contrary, access to social housing by asylum seekers and refugees is only marginally less difficult in the rest of the country than in London, although there is a crude surplus of social housing in most conurbations.

Equally significant to these broad geographical distinctions, and the concentration in conurbations, are more specific patterns of demand. Although patchy, a relatively small number of local authorities experience a particularly high level of demand from refugees and asylum seekers. These tend to be areas containing established communities to which specific refugee or asylum seekers belong or have an affinity, or are near ports of entry, or have other facilities or connection with the immigration process, for example, detention centres.

The wider context of housing provision

Our report is geared towards good practice implemented by RSLs. But this cannot be separated from either the role of local authorities in localities where RSLs have been active, nor from the role of Refugee Community-based Organisations (RCOs) which has expanded dramatically in the last few years. Responding to the curtailment of public sector assistance since 1996, a number of RSLs have made or have expanded provision, often in collaboration with the voluntary sector – notably with RCOs where there were often highly developed relationships – and local authorities' SSDs.

For these reasons, our study is set within this wider context. The scope and effectiveness of partnerships remain limited and problematic. Indeed, a key finding of our study is the need for improved partnership between the three sets of actors as fragmentation of service delivery has been one of the main consequences of changing policy and statutory provision.

Statutory context and The Housing Corporation's response

Historically, local authority housing departments have been the first point of access for refugees and asylum seekers needing accommodation. However, since the *1996 Asylum and Immigration Act* and the *1996 Housing Act* [throughout the report referred to as *the 1996 legislation*], the situation has become immeasurably more complex. The principal effect has been to deny local housing authorities the power to allocate non-qualifying asylum seekers council tenancies or homelessness assistance and to exclude asylum seekers from access to any public resources. As a result of a High Court judgment in October 1997, responsibility has subsequently fallen upon SSDs to secure shelter and sustenance within their obligations under the *1948 National Assistance Act* or the *1989 Children Act*. This ruling directed that intended government measures to withdraw all public assistance was inconsistent with the behaviour expected of a civilised country.

To fill the vacuum in supply, RSLs have extended their provision, often in partnership with SSDs. In contrast to local housing authorities, the outright ban has not directly applied to RSLs, who have been able to use discretion in deciding whether or not to offer housing. Here, though, guidance from The Housing Corporation, contained in two circulars, *R3 – 04/97*, 'Lettings to certain persons [from] abroad' (January 1997) and *R3 – 34/97*, 'Temporary lettings to asylum seekers' (January 1998), has been very cautious, emphasising risk over obligation. This has created uncertainty among RSLs, reinforcing their reluctance to engage this sector.

These circulars summarised the legislative implications for RSLs, of the two 1996 Acts, and the principal judicial decisions made under the *1948 National Assistance Act* and the *1989 Children Act*. The first circular warned about the impact of lettings to asylum seekers on the aims and objectives of the agency, and the financial risks of tenants who

might not have the means to pay rents and service charges. The second circular provided more encouraging guidance in the light of the courts' decisions in various appeal cases. This advised that RSLs could provide a small proportion of temporary lettings to asylum seekers, within the terms of Part VII of the *1996 Housing Act* or the *1948 National Assistance Act* or the *1989 Children Act*. It indicated the need and scope for arrangements with SSDs. Similar warnings were given about the need to ensure compliance with the aims and objectives of the RSL and the likely effect on grant recovery rules. While relaxing the guidance in the earlier circular, the net effect on RSL activity remains modest.

Provision has expanded but has not, as yet, dramatically increased, since the current system offers little incentive or security to RSLs. More than ever dependent on guaranteed income streams, offering housing to asylum seekers has become complicated and risky: it involves checks on immigration status, and the risk of arrears if an asylum seeker loses his/her case. The curtailment of benefits had a serious impact on RSLs' ability to operate as they had prior to the 1996 Acts, although this has been ameliorated by the availability of the *1948 National Assistance Act* funding through SSDs. Yet, with local authorities constrained in their ability to provide housing, and the private rented sector often uninterested in tenants whose finances are uncertain, RSLs, despite their own constraints, are undoubtedly best placed to offer help to refugees and asylum seekers.

Overview of findings

- Housing services to refugees and asylum seekers are increasingly provided by the RSL/voluntary sectors as a result of statutory and policy changes in the last three years. Given the continuing impact of the 1996 legislation, RSLs indicate a growth in demand and provision. The government's policy review proposals will expand the role of these two groups of agencies in the next few years.

- Although relatively few in number, there are some RSLs whose attitude and professionalism ensure that services for asylum seekers and refugees are positive, sensitive and reflect stated needs and aspirations. This good practice, detailed in Chapters 5 and 6 and with further recommendations in Chapter 8, offers a model for others to follow.

- Within a general typology of RSLs set out in Chapter 4, particular attention is paid to the specialist, refugee or minority ethnic and/or community-based RSLs and non-registered associations. These RSLs currently offer best practice to the communities they serve. This practice should be extended to other RSLs.

- Good practice, in the perception of asylum seeker and refugee tenants, is based on culturally sensitive service delivery. Aspects most valued are social factors including privacy, cultural and social activities, own language documents, and supportive staff.

- However, a considerable amount of practice fails to meet the standards generally deemed appropriate for RSLs. The lack of good practice is not directly attributed to RSLs alone, but in some cases to the organisations they work with or through.

- The main concerns of the tenants are: access and allocation policies which appear to discriminate against specific social and cultural needs; failure to provide accommodation and services responsive to the distinctive and diverse social and demographic characteristics of refugees and asylum seekers. These factors increase the sense of vulnerability, social exclusion and isolation.

- The shortfalls in RSL practice and the lack of institutional capacity, especially among RCOs, indicate significant training needs which are currently unfulfilled.

- Much more could be achieved at relatively little additional cost, to enhance the quality of service delivery by good practice RSLs and to improve, substantially, the poor practice.

- The skills and expertise of RCOs are substantially underutilised which means that consumers do not obtain the best services.

- While there is a lack of commitment generally by RSLs, this is most notable in the larger, urban associations, many of whom operate widely in areas where refugee and asylum seeker communities are concentrated. Although they have the resources and capacity to make provision, several reasons combine to create this neglect. These reasons apply to the field as a whole:

  - The influence of local authorities may marginalise this group. Their failure to prioritise asylum seeker and refugee needs, or the high level of local authority nominations, leave RSLs with little discretion.

  - The increasingly commercial orientation taken by RSLs and the perceived risks of accommodating groups such as asylum seekers whose ability to pay is uncertain.

  - The level of uncertainty surrounding refugee and asylum seeker policy and statute. This is critical, and is likely to remain so, even after the government's current review of policy.

  - Funding inequalities are a major factor explaining the variable level of services.

  - Political will in local authorities and public sensitivity condition the approach and visibility of the RSLs operating in this field. In some locations, activity appears to take place in spite of, rather than with the support and coordination of the local authority.

- A major consequence of the policy and statutory changes, especially since 1966, has been the increasing fragmentation of service delivery and a severe lack of coordination between the various actors. This is evident within local authorities, especially between housing and social services departments whose lead role is often unstructured and provision is poorly regulated. There is also a lack of cooperation and coordination by organisations (the RCOs) set up by and for refugee and asylum seeker communities. The piecemeal approach by RSLs contributes to this lack of concerted action.

- RSLs appear unusually reticent to claim ownership of good practice in this area. Instead, most prefer to maintain a low profile, perhaps prompted by their politically sensitive partners, and to avoid the obvious potential for controversy and unpopularity. This militates against the dissemination and sharing of good practice.

- While housing supply is nominally greater outside London and the south-east, and despite assumed differences between this region and the rest of the country, access to RSL housing by refugees and asylum seekers and performance and provision for them by RSLs, do not vary significantly between the three locations of the study. This challenges some of the common assumptions about the uniqueness of London's experience and the policy responses.

- Many of these problems arise from the volatility of policy, the uncertain status of many of the claimants, and the lack of clarity about the discretion available to RSLs to make provision for this group. These wider structural and resource constraints, and especially the government's policy review, are fundamental barriers to strategic responses and the adoption of good practice in housing provision for refugees and asylum seekers. These are crucial determinants of the findings and recommendations.

- Refugees and asylum seekers have little political leverage, either individually, or as a group, which makes them a low priority for resource allocation. As a result, they and the organisations representing them appear often resigned to low expectations, which are often met.

We intend this study to contribute to the work of many practitioners and advocates whose aim is to improve the lot of the thousands of people arriving in the UK seeking a place of refuge and who depend on their continuing assistance and support.

2

Research setting and research methods

Research context

Refugees and asylum seekers have attracted relatively little research until recently. Most of the research has been conducted among programme or quota refugees, such as Ugandan Asians and Vietnamese. There is much less research on spontaneous arrivals which have predominated in recent years and with whom our study is mainly concerned. The focus of much existing work is almost wholly on refugees or those with reasonably secure status, not asylum seekers – a distinctive element in our study.

Within this context, our study draws on and develops a number of themes. The full literature and research background are detailed in this chapter, in Appendix A and in the References and further reading.

Housing need and provision are consistently identified as a crucial element in refugee reception and settlement experiences (see, for example, Field, 1985; AMA, 1991; Carey Wood et al, 1995; Robinson, 1993a; RC, 1997b; 1997c). Good housing is as important as economic well-being in enabling refugees and asylum seekers to become part of the community (Carey-Wood et al, 1995, p 96).

The main findings from earlier research are:

- Housing provision for refugees should be set within the wider context of resettlement policies (Field, 1985; Robinson, 1993a).

- There has been little systematic research specifically on refugees and housing, beyond some operational needs (for example, HACT, 1994a; 1994b). Moreover, much of the research

predates the impact of the *1996 Asylum and Immigration* and *Housing Acts*.

- The distinctive needs of asylum seekers and refugees for resources such as housing, the problems of unequal access to housing experienced by this population, the poorer quality accommodation which they invariably occupy (HACT, 1994a), and the lack of choice (Humm, 1996), are important pointers to providers. There are distinctive patterns of housing need through time (Humm, 1996).

- Policy making is characterised by low levels of consultation by service providers with refugee groups; poor targeting of services to refugees; lack of awareness of refugees allows them to be sidelined in policy making (Robinson, 1998), which often neglects a strategic framework (Humm, 1996).

- Refugee Community-based Organisations (RCOs) play a vital role in the resettlement process (BRC, 1988). But their precarious and constrained existence, and the difficulty of linking well with mainstream housing providers, makes it difficult for them to become established partners or RSLs (HACT, 1994b).

- Coordination between local authorities, RSLs, the voluntary sector and RCOs is a key element in satisfactory provision (BRC, 1987; 1988).

- There is a perceived need for reception centres (BRC, 1987; Refugee Housing Association, 1997; RC, 1997c), though these need to be properly resourced and coordinated. Pragmatic and inadequate provision lead to problems of social isolation and marginalisation from the mainstream of social life (HACT, 1994b).

- The most extensive and systematic research on resettlement is that commissioned by the Home Office in 1995 (Carey Wood et al, 1995). It revealed that there may be poor knowledge of RSL provision on the part of refugees and that their perceptions may have been blurred by the negative experiences of some already in RSL accommodation (Carey Wood et al, 1995, p 68).

- Secondary migration, and the spatial concentration of refugee communities, is a characteristic of refugee settlement processes (Field, 1985; Robinson, 1993a, 1993b, 1998; Duke and Marshall, 1995; Joly, 1996). Government dispersal policies for earlier programme or quota refugees paradoxically accentuated these processes.

- Some degree of clustering is not only inevitable, but, if effectively organised, can encourage community formation and self-sufficiency (Joly, 1996).

Research methods

In reading this report, it is important to bear in mind some crucial qualifications about our research methods and the findings.

Because of the sensitivity of the subject and the difficulty of sampling refugees and asylum seekers, we have not adopted quantitative methods. Through a combination of questionnaire surveys of individuals and focus groups, we have tried to develop a qualitative picture of housing provision by RSLs and the study group's experience of it. The findings and recommendations should be read as guidance from our observations of and data collected from the various actors, not as a statistically robust sample of practice.

For these reasons, we cannot easily make claims for the generality of the findings as a whole. Nor can we correlate particular client group experiences with particular RSL practices. On the other hand, our study is rooted in the respondents' own insights and perceptions. It offers insights into how RSLs provide for the client group and the strengths and weaknesses of this provision. These elements are sufficiently representative to assist the development of best practice in provision and management.

Equally for the refugees and asylum seekers, the primary aim was to draw into our understanding of RSL provision and practice, their experiences and perspectives as tenants. Their views, and the RCOs which represent them, shed significant light on good and less satisfactory practices, policies and procedures of the RSLs. Because the sample used is small, caution should be exercised in making categorical conclusions from these data.

The conjuncture of refugee and asylum seeker perspectives and those of the RSL providers is an innovative aspect of this study.

Our study has also included information about local authorities (mainly housing and SSDs), since the specific role of RSLs fits within the wider context of housing policy and the role of these key actors in supply. In this way we establish a more comprehensive picture of the characteristics of local demand and supply, the policy framework, the strengths and limitations of the various actors, the range and type of supporting networks, and the development of partnerships between the various actors to meet the needs of refugees and asylum seekers.

Our field work was conducted in London (London Boroughs of Newham and Tower Hamlets), Birmingham (City) and Manchester (City). Although the substantial majority of asylum seekers and refugees live in London, this fact, combined with the enormous pressures on housing stock in London, creates what is assumed to be an untypical picture of the housing processes for asylum seekers and refugees in much of the rest of the country. For this reason, while including London, we wished to examine provision elsewhere, with different refugee groups and different housing contexts, but recognising that the focus should be large metropolitan centres.

Research methods – service providers

Our approach was conducted in two stages.

Postal survey

We conducted a short postal questionnaire survey in England which included about 500 active registered RSLs, 250 urban-based local housing authorities and about 200 RCOs. Response rates were 25%, 20% and 10% respectively. The aim of this brief survey was to scope the study in terms of the extent to which refugees and asylum seekers represented significant and special need; the impact of the 1996 legislation on policies and procedures; range of housing provision; numbers accommodated; partnerships and networks. The data collected from this survey enabled us to focus on some of the key issues which emerged, and to target our selection of localities, service providers and organisations with more confidence.

Main survey

The main survey of service providers collected sample data, in each of the three localities, from RSLs, RCOs and local authority professionals.

In all, 26 **RSLs** were contacted, comprising a range of providers (general needs, community-oriented and special needs including specific refugee housing associations, whether registered or not) who were active in housing for refugees and asylum seekers. Interviews, using open-ended questions, were then conducted with senior staff from each RSL.

The interviews were structured around key variables such as: the nature and scope of involvement with refugees and asylum seekers; context of provision; networks and partnerships; specialist services and support offered.

Refugee community-based organisations (RCOs), interviews were conducted with key representatives, again using an open-ended question format. Data were collected on many issues, for example, the origins and history of the organisation; the role and functions; its specific role and functions with regard to housing and RSLs; networking with other organisations, local authorities and so on.

In addition to the 19 RCOs contacted, we also conducted group interviews with members of specific community groups who, where possible, were also RSL tenants. We conducted a one-day 'focus group' workshop involving about 15 London-based RCOs in a structured exchange of comparative experiences on issues such as empowerment and participation; how partnerships

were formed; and the extent to which RCOs were able to engage with the RSLs.

For the **local authorities**, interviews were conducted with officers in housing and SSDs. These interviews followed an open question format with the aims of establishing the role of the local authorities in allocation referral and support services for refugee and asylum seekers, especially with regard to housing provision; local authority policies with regard to this group; and networks and partnership with other housing service providers.

Research methods – refugees and asylum seekers

The second element of the research was to examine the provision of RSL accommodation from the perspectives of the tenants and to gain an insight into their experiences. Questionnaire survey methods were combined with ethnographic research in the three case study locations. A clustered sample frame was used and access was gained through either RSLs or local RCOs.

Our sample is limited to existing RSL tenants. This creates some boundaries to our data, but has prevented us gaining potentially valuable insights from those who have exited from RSL tenancies.

Scope of the data on refugees and asylum seekers

Face-to-face interviews were conducted with 46 tenant households. While comparatively small and not fully representative, the sample nonetheless reflects the diversity of refugee and asylum seeker communities – status, ethnic/national origin, levels of self-sufficiency and complex household composition.

Primary data were collected by a structured questionnaire survey (see Appendix D), comprising both closed and open questions, seeking both qualitative and quantitative information. The main aims were to investigate how refugees and asylum seekers gained access to RSL accommodation; the client group's experience of the housing processes and the roles and responsibilities of the RSLs; the quality and scope of the services provided and how well client group needs were understood; support services and meeting individual needs, for example, counselling, training and employment, and social and community needs; levels of empowerment and participation; and the relationship between housing needs and housing provision at different stages of the resettlement process.

The tenant interview data were supplemented by a small number of 'group' interviews. These focused on the housing situation of specific ethnic groups of refugees, rather than the particular experience of individual households.

3

Existing provision for refugees and asylum seekers

The housing providers

The national backdrop

As a result of the statutory and policy changes in the last three years, housing services to refugees and asylum seekers are increasingly provided by organisations located in the RSL/voluntary sectors. Nevertheless, our nationwide postal survey indicates that only a relatively small number of organisations are currently active. Given the impact of the 1996 legislation, RSLs indicate a growth in demand and provision. To the extent that the government's policy review proposals will accentuate the role of these two groups of agencies, the patterns we describe are likely to expand and predominate in the next few years.

The main providers are located in urban areas containing the greatest refugee concentrations. But the substantial variation in the environment in which housing organisations operate across the country produces considerable diversity of service provision for refugees and asylum seekers. This is exemplified in our three main case study areas of London, Birmingham and Manchester, each of which is described in greater detail later in this report (Chapter 5). In London and the South East, there is substantial over-demand for social housing, especially with regard to households accepted as homeless. In most urban areas in the rest of the country there is a crude surplus of supply over demand, and the issue is less of quantity and more of quality.

This regional imbalance has been a major influence on the organisations active in each area and the style of approach they have chosen to adopt with regard to refugees and asylum seekers. In London the strategic fragmentation between the 32 boroughs has created a policy vacuum within and between those areas most affected by refugee and asylum seeker activity. This contrasts with the situation elsewhere. In some respects, the situation in London has been beneficial, offering scope for the emergence and development of community-based voluntary groups and organisations. In the boroughs where the local authority has a well-developed strategy for working in partnership with the voluntary sector, this can be effective. However, in many areas the response is a patchwork of small interest groups operating in ad hoc capacities with little coordination. In a number of instances, far from receiving support and guidance from local authorities, such groups often appear to operate in open conflict against the politics of local resource allocation procedures and policies.

The overall lack of a systematic or well thought out approach to the housing needs of refugees and asylum seekers impacts negatively on those whose leverage on resources and whose eligibility for welfare assistance is, in any case, very restricted. Like so many minority ethnic households, the life chances of refugees and asylum seekers exist in the most deprived areas of the country. This not only disadvantages them, but also casts further deprivation upon the already overstretched and under-resourced local public services.

Even in areas of surplus, the actual provision of housing for this client group and the coordination of service provision appears to be no more satisfactory than in areas of greater deprivation and housing shortfall.

Who are the providers?

Most of the organisations we have surveyed fall into one of the five categories identified in Table 1. These distinctions are rather general, although they reflect an emphasis and ethos commonly represented in each organisational category. In some cases an organisation spans more than one category. There are also overlaps between RCOs and housing associations which are not registered with The Housing Corporation. In many cases, these are primarily community groups which have developed a housing function.

Organisations within the same category do not necessarily follow identical patterns of service delivery. There are considerable differences, even in the detail of day-to-day service delivery, resulting from a combination of internal and external factors. There is substantial variation in the performance and effectiveness of organisations working with refugees and asylum seekers. We define effectiveness in terms of the success in meeting policy objectives and the quality of the services delivered to users. The scope of variation in practice and the reasons for it are discussed in Chapters 4, 5 and 6.

An important issue for our study was whether particular types of organisation are better placed than others to offer the services needed by refugees and asylum seekers. Are the special needs of these households best served through specialist organisations set up specifically for this purpose? In this context, the majority of organisations we identified in categories 5 and 6 in Table 1 are staffed and managed by workforces representative of the communities they serve. It might therefore be expected that such organisations offer the empathy, specialist knowledge and language skills which can most effectively support their service users. There is little doubt that for many refugees and asylum seekers, these services represent important responses to their very real needs as our survey of the tenants in the next chapter shows.

Against this, we have found that the more generic RSLs (ie category 1) can usually offer a greater range of housing management skills and resources, delivered through staff who are trained and supported in this area of work. However, there is a concern that more generic associations might possibly be involved with asylum seekers primarily because they perceived a lucrative development opportunity, rather than a commitment to the client group.

Does empathy outweigh expertise? There cannot be a categorical answer to this question. Thus, in Table 2, we have attempted to provide a typology of organisational characteristics in order to elaborate in more detail the relative strengths and weaknesses of the six main organisational categories.

As with Table 1, these are broad generalisations. It is also important to note that the characteristics identified relate specifically to the skills and experience in dealing with refugees and asylum seekers, rather than as a broader assessment of the organisations' capabilities overall.

Table 1: Categories of organisations offering services to refugees and asylum seekers

Type

1 General needs RSLs

2 Community-focused general needs RSLs (ie organisations with a strong cultural and operational bias towards Housing Plus initiatives, etc)

3 Specialist RSLs

4 Black and Minority Ethnic (BME) RSLs

5 Refugee-specific RSLs

6 Refugee and/or community-based, housing associations (not registered with The Housing Corporation)

Table 2: Typology of organisations acting as landlord to refugees and asylum seekers

Type	Characteristics	Typical strengths	Potential drawbacks
General needs RSL	Diversity in terms of size (1-20,000+ dwellings) and objectives. Most active associations have a significant level of expertise in managing a social business. The major differences relate usually to available resources and constitutional aims.	Good housing management skills. Expert in all aspects of organisational management. Development and procurement expertise. Financial skills.	Generalised, may not understand needs of refugees and asylum seekers. Unlikely to have specialist skills in this area. May not offer holistic approach to housing, ie Housing Plus approach. May be perceived as remote by some parts of community.
Community-based general needs RSLs	Very similar to general needs associations in terms of structures. However, tend to be different in approach. More likely to have tenant involvement, develop Housing Plus initiatives and work in close partnership with a range of small, community groups.	Good housing management skills. Expert in all aspects of organisational management. Good networking skills with community. Preparedness to innovation and responsiveness. Local presence.	May not have the depth of resources of some of the larger general needs associations. Costs of provision may be higher than larger RSLs. Unlikely to have language skills or directly represent all groups they work with.
Specialist RSLs	Vary in size, but usually much smaller than general needs associations. Often focused on services for either elderly, single people or community care. Likely to manage hostels and shared accommodation rather than single family dwellings.	Skills in managing shared housing. More sensitive to diverse needs. May have expertise in reception and resettlement work. Close links into voluntary sector. Good fundraising skills.	May be too general in range of needs catered for; ie centred on a specific category of need rather than needs of refugees, etc. Unlikely to have language skills or directly represent all groups they work with.
BME and refugee-specific RSLs	Relatively small in number and size, perhaps with a leaning to one or more specific minority ethnic communities. Smaller ones may depend on larger associations for agency services, eg development. Workforce may be predominantly, but not necessarily exclusively, from ethnic minorities.	Good housing management skills. Expert in most aspects of organisational management. Good networking skills with community. Empathy with client group. May have language skills.	Unlikely to have the depth of resources of some of the larger general needs associations. May find it hard to compete against larger associations. Costs of provision may be higher than larger RSLs. Not always representative of communities they serve.
Refugee-specific RCOs	Tend to be small, community-based organisations. May be registered as Industrial and Provident Societies, but often not by The Housing Corporation. Likely to be very focused in location and client group.	Empathy with client group. Specialist cultural and religious knowledge. Language skills. Small, flexible, committed, dynamic.	Little training, particularly in housing management. Limited skills in networking. May be driven by local politics rather than actual needs or skills.

What is clear is that there are pros and cons in each of the organisational types listed above. For some communities, the idea of working with any organisation which did not have a clear local identity and could not demonstrate an empathy with their language, culture and religious foundations would be unthinkable. In many cases, such organisations also fulfil a broader role within the community, often acting as pressure groups and providing a focus for community development. In some cases, they have successfully integrated their focus on community issues with a structured and professional approach to housing management. But in many cases, this latter role has not been successfully completed, particularly in terms of training and skill development.

In contrast, the larger mainstream associations have housing management experience but in many cases lack understanding and empathy towards refugees and asylum seekers. However, there are two exceptions to this situation. The first relates to those RSLs, generally excluding the very largest, which have adopted an ethos of community focus and a commitment to the delivery of services which reflect the sentiments of Housing Plus. Such organisations usually have an infrastructure more readily able to work in constructive partnership with local organisations representing minority interests. They are therefore usually able to combine the benefits of professional housing management with a range of sensitive and supportive services for their consumers.

The second exception relates to the increasing use of hostel accommodation, usually for single asylum seekers who are assisted by SSDs under the *1948 National Assistance Act*. A number of RSLs with considerable experience in managing direct access housing and temporary accommodation have worked alongside local authorities and community groups to provide often quite large hostels combining both housing and related services. The main benefit of such arrangements has been the ability to offer assistance to a relatively large number of individuals at one time, using economies of scale to sustain the support services needed by residents. However, the use of large hostels is not without drawbacks, which are examined in Chapter 5.

The importance of partnerships and collaboration

In addition to the individual characteristics of the organisations involved with refugees and asylum seekers, the linkages and relationships between them are also important. Few of the smaller RSLs and community groups are able to act independently of the more established RSLs and local authorities. It is often the viability of these relationships which dictates the effectiveness of the services ultimately delivered.

Four partnership models cover most of the arrangements we have examined:

- RSLs adopting an incremental approach, incorporating and integrating refugee/asylum seeker issues within their work. These invariably appear more aware of, and better placed to respond to their clients' needs and usually work in close partnership with local RCOs to provide specialist support.
- RSLs working within agency agreements with voluntary sector groups. This often involves passing the day-to-day management of accommodation to specialist groups representing refugees and asylum seekers.
- RSLs developing and/or allocating existing housing to refugees and asylum seekers. In this model, housing management is usually carried out by the RSL. Specialist support, advice and advocacy skills are brought in where required.
- RSLs drawn into providing housing and/or support by default. These tend to be associations which have received ad hoc contacts by organisations such as the Red Cross in response to a particular crisis. Partnership arrangements are pragmatic and less integrated.

No one model stands out as better than another. Each has a place and offers similar prospects of success or failure. Which model proves most effective depends largely on the location, client group and constituent partners. What is critically important is that the terms of the partnership are clearly constructed, each party is aware of its obligations and responsibilities, and that there are clear mechanisms for monitoring whether the partnership is working. In many of the arrangements we examined one or more of these principles was missing or ineffective.

What is provided?

Two key areas of provision form the basis of the services delivered by organisations dealing with refugees and asylum seekers: advocacy, advice and support; and the provision of shelter itself (ie housing, hostel accommodation etc).

Support and advocacy

Many of the RCOs heavily involved with refugees and asylum seekers either started life or continue to perceive their primary function as the provision of service, support and advocacy, focusing on cultural, religious and language issues. These are often vital, not only to those newly arrived in a country, but also to existing members of the community who may need ongoing support and assistance.

It is often the issues which emerge from this work which motivate some RCOs to extend their range of services and become housing associations (whether registered or not). In such instances the relationship between the two components of support and housing provision generally combine in the delivery of a type of Housing Plus approach encouraged by The Housing Corporation. In this study, support and advocacy are only investigated insofar as they directly affect and relate to housing provision.

Housing

The housing options for refugees and asylum seekers have varied over recent years, depending on location, circumstances and timing, especially in relation to the impact of the *1996 Housing Act*.

While temporary accommodation has become the focus for much of the more recent housing for asylum seekers, residential options are spread across all tenures (see Table 3).

The data are not strictly comparable as they are drawn from different surveys carried out with different samples, and so on. However, they indicate a general pattern of distribution across tenures and the differences which exist between specific refugee groups. Briefly described below are the main alternative sources of accommodation available for such households.

1 Bed and Breakfast – used increasingly since the High Court judgment in 1997 (*R v Newham. LBC ex parte Medical Foundation and others, 1997*). SSDs suddenly found themselves with the responsibility to secure accommodation for thousands of single, destitute asylum seekers, having had no previous experience of the rehousing function.

This led to an explosion in the demand for Bed and Breakfast places, particularly in Central London. Feedback from voluntary groups working in the area indicates that many unsuitable dwellings were, and continue to be, used to cope with the demand.

Table 3: Tenure surveys of refugees and asylum seekers

Tenure	Horn of Africa Refugee Study, 1997[1]	Latin American Refugee Study, 1997[2]	Refugees in Newham Study, 1996[3]	Iraqi Community Study, 1996[4]	Refugee Council Study, 1989[5]	Home Office Study, 1995[6]
Private renting	19.2	34	54	42.4	23.7	25
Local authority	41	21	23	18.7	34.3	37
RSL	17.5	8	13	9.7	20.7	20
Temporary housing	17.2	26	na	na	8.9	na
Family/friends/other	2.2	11	3	4.7	4.3	6
Owner-occupiers	2.8	na	7	24.5	8.1	12

[1] Bariso (1997)
[2] Borkum (1997)
[3] Bloch (1996b)
[4] Iraqi Community Association (1996)
[5] BRC (1989)
[6] Carey-Wood et al (1995)

2 Hostels – hostels have played a large part in providing housing, usually for single asylum seekers. RSLs such as the YMCA, English Churches and St Mungo's, each with considerable experience in managing such establishments, have successfully provided such accommodation.

There are clearly divided views about appropriate maximum size for hostel accommodation. There is a fear that larger facilities might institutionalise the resettlement process, adding to the stress experienced by many traumatised asylum seekers. The experiences of a number of the hostel staff interviewed for this study appears to concur with this view, favouring smaller hostels as a means of providing better working environments for successful resettlement. An additional advantage is that small hostels tend to provoke less antagonism in obtaining planning permission and less racial tension in the area.

Asylum seekers living in hostels varied in their views. Some expressed preferences for larger or medium-sized hostels where they were able to become less visible and retain privacy. For example, one asylum seeker interviewed felt that hostel staff knew everything about him, even what book he was reading! Given his experience of persecution and lack of trust in officialdom, he inevitably felt threatened.

There is therefore a trade-off between achieving the economies of scale as against the delivery of quality support services and effective resettlement work. Very small hostels tend to be too small to sustain the cost of providing intensive services and are usually limited in their scope. We identified a number of worrying shortfalls in the support structures in many smaller hostel units, highlighting the need for improved assessment for, and the coordination of, peripatetic or floating support.

3 Short life property – many of the smaller, community organisations have been dependent on the availability of short life accommodation to house their clients. This was made possible by the availability of Mini-Housing Association Grant (HAG) from The Housing Corporation which enabled associations to bring properties back into use which had at least a two-year life. However,

with the reduction in capital spending and with abandonment of clearance and road schemes, the supply of suitable dwellings has largely dried up. This has already affected many RCOs and the situation promises to become even more acute in the future. In a study conducted among RCOs in London (HACT, 1994b), up to a third of the surveyed refugee groups' housing stock was under threat of withdrawal.

While offering the option to gain access to property for groups who would otherwise have none, the use of short life housing has not always been positive. Many dwellings falling into this category are in poor condition, located in run-down areas and in need of major investment. Often this is beyond the resources of the associations taking them on with the consequence of producing a poor living environment for any prospective tenant. However, it is often the case that such is the desperation of those needing accommodation, and so low are their expectations, that they will take anything.

4 Private rented sector – prior to the *1996 Asylum and Immigration Act*, the private rented sector was a main provider for many asylum seekers. Entitlement to housing benefit meant that asylum seekers had discretion to obtain their own accommodation. This is now not possible, and many of those previously resident in the private rented sector have had to relocate to accommodation sponsored by SSDs. This, of course, has important implications for the self-sufficiency of asylum seekers, and their capacity to regain their autonomy and independence.

5 Accommodation out of area – a small number of local authorities, mainly in London, have been compelled by the pressure on local housing stock, to use temporary accommodation out of area to provide a service to refugees and asylum seekers. Newham, for example, entered into an agreement to utilise property in Eastbourne. The justification for 'exporting' households has been the lack of availability of suitable accommodation within the local authority area, and cost, since accommodation is cheaper elsewhere. Of course, this practice fragments the social and community networks which are so vital to asylum seekers and refugees in the early stages of the resettlement process and increases the marginalisation they experience.

This is largely the strategic approach taken by the government, however, in the White Paper, *Fairer, faster and firmer*, which proposes locating asylum seekers where accommodation is available rather than having regard to their needs or support networks.

6 Permanent accommodation – permanent accommodation, through RSLs for example, is only really an option for *qualifying persons*, that is, those who have official leave to stay in the country. Local authorities also have duties under the *1989 Children Act* which may involve providing housing for households with young children.

7 Owner-occupation – owner-occupation relates specifically to refugees rather than asylum seekers. Comprising a relatively small percentage of this group, there appear to be varied patterns in terms of length of stay and country of origin.

Summary

Housing occupied by refugees and asylum seekers is diverse. Although, obviously, the opportunities open to them since the *1996 Asylum and Immigration Act* have narrowed and overall provision is more limited, a significant range of options remains. Whether all of these offer a comparable level of service quality and consistency is less clear as the next two chapters explain. In many cases, asylum seekers have little choice but to accept the accommodation available in their immediate vicinity. This may result in a positive experience, particularly if the available housing is supplemented with strong community support. However, in other cases, the outcomes are much less satisfactory. The reasons for this are examined in greater detail in the following chapters.

Perceptions and experiences of refugees and asylum seekers in RSL property

Introduction

In conducting the study, we interviewed a sample of 46 RSL tenants to gain a user perspective of housing provision. This was supplemented by a small number of 'group' interviews and data collected from representatives of RCOs. The characteristics of the sample have already been described in Chapter 2.

This chapter summarises the findings from the survey. Appendix B provides a detailed account of the responses of the refugees and asylum seekers.

Characteristics of the sample

The sample interviewed covered 11 ethnic/national groups, of whom 33% were asylum seekers and 13% with full refugee status; the remainder were in other temporary categories. Over two thirds were receiving benefit and less than 10% were in full-time work. Just over 50% of the sample comprised single-person households and 33% comprised single-headed households. Over 50% of the sample had arrived less than two years prior to the interview. Just under two thirds of the sample were resident in the two London boroughs of our survey, a quarter in Birmingham and the balance in Manchester.

Twenty-two respondents, or 48% of the sample, were living in flats, 11 in shared houses, another 11 lived in hostels (three in rooms and eight in bedsits) and two were in a reception centre in Birmingham.

Experience of current RSL accommodation

The key issues to emerge from the survey were as follows:

Access

- The two main reasons for living in the present accommodation were availability of housing by moving into the present area (39% of respondents); and proximity to family or friends (13 respondents – 28%).

- Moreover, 48% had found their present accommodation through friends and relatives. The desire to regroup in co-ethnic communities appears to be a significant characteristic in the housing process.

- The main issue in relation to obtaining accommodation is the length of time respondents had to wait to be housed. Fourteen respondents complained of problems in this respect (30% of the sample). A minority has waited for up to three years to find accommodation!

- Allocation procedures, in the few cases where RSLs operate points systems, are seen as arbitrary and open to manipulation by housing managers. The process is perceived to be overly bureaucratic and unfair in its effects. More generally, the lack of choice is resented.

These findings emphasise the need for enhanced sensitivity in access and allocation procedures by RSLs.

Problems with accommodation

- The survey finds that half the sample had no problems with their accommodation.

- Nearly half the sample (43%) have experienced problems with their accommodation – repairs and overcrowding forming the most common complaints. Other issues include insufficient security, racial harassment and poor attitudes of support staff. Of the tenants who had experienced problems, there is a balance between those who found responses helpful and those who did not. The majority finding their landlords helpful are either in refugee community RSLs or recently arrived asylum seekers with close personal relations with support staff. This suggests that tenants value contact with landlords or support staff which provides either cultural affinity or a sense of belonging. In the unhelpful/very unhelpful category, all are from tenants in mainstream RSL properties.

- The most common sources of tension are issues of bureaucracy, delays in repairs and autocratic managerial styles. There is concern at the lack of familiarity with complaints procedures in RSLs. Women tenants also complain of the difficulties in sharing with men.

- Female single-headed households face particular financial difficulties. This is attributable mainly to the problem of balancing childcare needs with part-time work, when they come off benefits, while at the same time earning enough to pay what they often contend to be excessively high rents in RSL properties. These problems are not unique to RSLs, but bear on wider RSL financial policies and the pressures to sustain a guaranteed rental income stream from their tenants.

- While only 33% of the respondents explicitly replied to the question on aspects they value most in their accommodation, the responses indicate that social factors including privacy, the provision of cultural and social activities and friendly staff, as well as own language documentation, are the most significant. Approximately 30% of respondents indicate that additional services they would most like to be provided by RSLs were social and cultural events or activities.

This evidence points to the need for good practice to deliver improved management systems to handle problems with accommodation, provide information and advice, review rent levels and residents' ability to pay and ensure that there are effective procedures to handle complaints. Best practice in these areas must be targeted to the specific needs of refugees and asylum seekers and must be sensitive to the cultural and gender issues which are of concern to them.

Social isolation

- Although not unique to RSLs, overcoming social isolation in housing is one of the most significant experiences of the respondents. It compounds the more general experience of social exclusion experienced by refugees and asylum seekers.

- Social isolation is a common experience among women, accentuated by lack of familiarity with welfare systems, distance from extended family networks, and with sometimes higher levels of illiteracy (eg Somali women).

- Elderly refugees are also particularly vulnerable to isolation, with few or no relatives remaining in their home countries to which they can return, and as the young people move away from the community living in exile. Those interviewed place great store on the social events organised by their RSLs, regarding this as among the best aspects of their accommodation.

Over and above the marginality of many minority groups, the specific social and personal experiences of forced migrants – family separation, loss of homeland, life-long memories of trauma – highlight the sensitivity which is needed in supporting refugees and asylum seekers. To the extent that RSLs claim expertise in catering for minority groups who are often marginalised, these factors underline the obligation on them to develop appropriate policies and practices. These should be responsive to the unique social and cultural experiences and situations which these tenants confront in order to combat isolation and exclusion.

Within the refugee and asylum seeker population there are important sub-groups, such as women and elderly people, which are an important group in their own right with their own distinct needs.

Overall, while reassuringly there is little evidence of bad practice, there are a number of key pointers to the ways in which RSLs can develop more responsive and sensitive policies and management structures with regard to this tenant group.

Participation

- Thirty out of the 46 respondents (65%) were aware of regular tenants' meetings, but only 19 have attended in the past (41% of the total sample). The main reasons for non-attendance are lack of interest, work commitments, lack of information and in only one case is 'unfriendly management' given as a reason.

- The majority who attended found the meetings very successful, a response commonly associated with general satisfaction with the accommodation and perceptions of already feeling included in the running of their RSLs. Reasons given for the lack of success in meetings vary from a perception of management tokenism, to inactivity and conflict among tenants themselves.

The high success rate of meetings may be attributable to a degree of self-selection of the participants. Moreover, the survey did not investigate more complex issues of empowerment. Nevertheless, there is some positive evidence that some RSLs recognise the importance of participation by refugee tenants and adopt measures to facilitate this.

The obvious requirement is for RSLs to enhance ways of working with their refugee and asylum seeker tenants which further encourage participation and involvement. How non-participants can best be encouraged, individually or in groups, to become more involved in the running of their accommodation, is a major priority. Social and cultural events and a sensitivity to particular ethnic or cultural factors, such as own language documents, are positive factors which stimulate participation and involvement in the residential community.

Identified improvements in RSL performance

Apart from improvements to performance which can be deduced from responses by the refugees and asylum seekers, the following are specifically highlighted in their responses.

- Ten out of 27 respondents indicate greater participation and cooperation between tenants as the most significant factors.

- Other factors include the provision of more information; own language materials; reduction in waiting lists; and the encouragement of better staff–tenant relationships.

- In hostels in particular, there is a perceived need for greater independence, for example, a lifting of restrictions on visiting times and the provision of social and cultural events to overcome the effects of isolation.

These responses bear out the conclusions in the previous section, that a sense of integration and control over one's environment is one of the principle factors in the perception of well-being among refugee and asylum seeker tenants.

Conclusions

Despite misgivings and criticisms of RSLs, overall, the refugees and asylum seekers interviewed recognise the benefits and appreciate the provision by RSLs. The majority appear reasonably satisfied with the physical accommodation, its maintenance and quality, especially where privacy is respected.

That effective resettlement comes through a sense of autonomy and control over one's environment is a principle factor in the perception of well-being among those refugee and asylum seeker tenants satisfied with RSL properties. This has important implications for the way RSLs enable their tenants through participation, social and culturally sensitive support services, and management practices which reflect the particular needs and experiences of this group.

The availability of RSL accommodation and the positive experiences of refugee and asylum seeker tenants seem to stimulate the well-documented process of secondary migration. This will accentuate rising demand for RSL accommodation, together with statutory and national policy trends. It has very significant implications for RSLs in terms of the tenant mix of minority specialist needs and, consequently, letting practices, and management and support services they will need to offer.

While acknowledging the limitations of the small sample, nevertheless, there are significant pointers indicating how RSLs can develop policies and improve practice for this group of tenants. Enhancing the quality of housing service and management, and providing accommodation and support better attuned to their needs, requires proper resourcing and a comprehensive rather than an incremental approach which has been largely adopted to date.

Refugees and asylum seekers have an array of distinctive yet diverse social and demographic characteristics which may increase their sense of vulnerability and heighten their sense of social exclusion and isolation. These aspects are not fully taken into account by RSLs, in the perception of the respondents, even in the best practice RSLs. This provides very significant indicators of the ways in which RSLs need to develop sensitive and well conceived policies and practices for management and service support which recognise these unique characteristics.

Bad practice is not widespread, at least in the experience of the respondents. But substantial improvements in and the sensitising of existing practice are required. The extremely variable standards of performance and the lack of specific provision tailored to the needs of particular refugee and asylum seeker groups indicate a limited appreciation of the diversity of need expressed by this group.

5

Case studies – patterns and lessons

Introduction

This section describes the findings from the three case study locations – Manchester, Birmingham and the London Boroughs of Newham and Tower Hamlets. It explores the main issues under three main headings: the local authority policy frameworks and coordinating mechanisms; perspectives from a selection of refugee community groups and community-based housing associations and RSLs; and an overview of generic issues which span the sector but which are principally derived from RSLs and also RCOs.

Despite assumed differences, housing performance and provision by RSLs for refugees and asylum seekers did not vary significantly between the three locations of our study. Anticipation that services would be better delivered and coordinated outside London – where public sector housing policy and provision is fragmented across the London boroughs – is not borne out in the study. Local authority or RSL performance is not significantly different.

While housing shortfalls are nominally less outside London, from the experience of the asylum seekers, it is not evident that RSL accommodation is more readily accessible outside the capital.

These findings challenge some of the common assumptions about the uniqueness of London's experience and the policy responses.

Local authority policy frameworks, coordination and networking

RSL provision for asylum seekers and refugees, as for all tenant groups, takes place within the framework of local authority housing policies and strategies, and the coordinating mechanisms and networks established to assist the implementation of those policies.

A distinctive feature in both Manchester and Birmingham, in contrast to the London boroughs surveyed, is the proactive policies of these authorities. They have conducted corporate and comprehensive policy reviews of service provision for refugees and asylum seekers. In contrast, many of the London boroughs, including our two case study boroughs, have adopted a more reactive approach to what is often perceived, politically, to be a highly sensitive issue.

- Despite the contrasts with the London boroughs, corporate strategies in both Birmingham and Manchester have not significantly improved the quality of service delivery. Housing provision for asylum seekers is now effectively determined by national legislation. Even given political commitment, local authorities have little discretion.

- In shifting the burden from housing to SSDs, the 1996 legislation has introduced needless competition between two departments. Initiatives by SSDs are innovative; but they are ad hoc, reactive, not coordinated across the authority, and are not regulated with the same quality control measures applied by housing departments.

- Initial improvements to liaison stimulated by major strategic policy reviews have not sustained effective partnerships and coordination with other agencies and service providers or with community-based groups.

- Liaison with refugee community-based organisations, through joint working groups comprising local authorities and community/ voluntary agencies, has not been sustained. There is a sense of fragmented effort and duplication; but this can be overcome where a thriving voluntary sector is encouraged by the local authority (eg in Oxford where we conducted supplementary field work).

- RSLs and unregistered housing associations working with refugees and asylum seekers present a similarly uncoordinated picture. Without central policy direction, RSLs have often acted opportunistically and reactively. The effect has been a patchwork of practice; this is particularly acute in London.

These negative impressions do not deny the existence of good practice: there are initiatives which are exemplars for others to follow and these are detailed in the following chapter. Nor are the organisations which house asylum seekers necessarily to blame for the current situation, although there are many aspects where performance and practice need improvement. The overwhelming problem is one of a national policy vacuum which we address at the end of the report.

Perspectives from various refugee community groups and community-based housing associations and RSLs

RCOs in the case study locations – patterns and organisation

- On the whole, poorly organised and resourced community organisations and the networks they provide are vital elements in sustaining group

identity and gaining access to housing for refugees and asylum seekers.

- The presence or absence of a settled refugee community is only one factor among many which determines the character of housing need for refugee communities and the extent to which these communities are formally organised.

- RCOs in London tend to be organised around national groups of asylum seekers and refugees, although degrees of formal community organisation vary. Many refugees may be present in an area but not be formally organised.

- Variations in policy and practice of the major housing providers across London make it very difficult for RCOs to resource concerted involvement across the metropolis. Their presence may thus appear to be more patchy than is the case.

- Probably reflecting the smaller number of refugees and asylum seekers in Manchester and Birmingham, multi-national umbrella organisations are more evident. Independent refugee organisations are, as yet, less active and less well established. Their tenuous existence limits their influence on the policies and practices of the major providers such as RSLs.

- The stance of the local authority – proactive or not – is a significant factor in refugee community formation and the role it plays on behalf of the refugees and asylum seekers.

A range of specific issues emerged from the main refugee communities in the sample. There is variation between groups and the locations of their tenancies. What follows is only representative of the particular situation of each of the groups. Nonetheless, there are some tentative conclusions which will help RSLs to develop best practice in response to these experiences.

Tamils in Newham

From the Tamil Housing Association (founded in 1986) there are three significant findings relevant to the policies and practices of RSLs.

- Specialist needs and support are best provided by those with inside knowledge of the community being served. RSL refugee workers are thought to be under pressure to follow bureaucratic rules in the large RSLs and less sensitive to tenants' needs.

- The need to address housing provision for different stages in the settlement process is critical. More hostel accommodation is required and move-on housing is essential as personal circumstances – marriage, greater independence, becoming elderly etc – of refugees and asylum seekers change.

- A central objective in housing provision must be to promote self-sufficiency and independence.

Somalis in Tower Hamlets

The main influx of Somalis began in 1988 when the civil war escalated in Somalia. The community, although initially ill-equipped to deal with the growing influxes, has been developing its capacity with a variety of initiatives. There are two points drawn from this community group.

- Specialist needs and support are critical. This is exemplified by the formation of Karin Housing Association (unregistered) in 1988 by Somalis, which is well placed to respond to the specific needs at different stages of the settlement process, because it is Somali-run. Advice, assistance and support are integral aspects of the work of Karin.

- There is an example of successful partnership between the community and an RSL. A sheltered housing scheme for elderly Somalis in the Isle of Dogs, now solely managed by East Thames Housing Trust (ETHG), provides a range of services, including housing and welfare advice and health referrals. A management committee consists of statutory organisations, health authorities, the local law centre, the ETHG and Praxis (a local voluntary organisation working with refugees which was instrumental in setting up the hostel).

The Polish Parish Committee and Mosscare, Manchester

This example illustrates an RSL, responsive to the 'accidental' location of refugees in a community, developing partnership initiatives with community groups to provide for local needs. As with the Somali example, effective partnership and specialist

support are key elements of this innovative scheme involving Mosscare Housing Association and the Polish community. The scheme, which dates from 1986, tackles the housing needs of a sizeable community of elderly Polish refugees.

- A joint scheme has been developed by the two partners providing 50 flats for elderly people of both Polish and mainstream communities. Specialist care and support is provided by the Polish community – family and religious ties are seen as important components of this support.

- The implications for housing providers of long-term change in housing needs are also significant aspects of this example. Demand for specialist long-term provision and intensive personal care for elderly refugee groups with unique demographic and ethnic characteristics is likely to increase with the protracted settlement of refugee populations which are, at present, relatively new arrivals by comparison. Scope for repatriation and reintegration may decline and the aging groups may become more socially isolated. This scheme shows how the imposition of changing demands has been met by flexible and adapative provision and support services of the RSL built into strategic plans.

Bosnians in Birmingham

In contrast to the other refugee groups in this study, the Bosnians are programme or quota refugees – estimated to be about 400 in Birmingham. From this example two main factors emerge.

- The value of coordination and community solidarity has enabled the Bosnian community in Birmingham, the largest outside London, to settle more quickly than is characteristic of many asylum seekers even though they do not have full refugee status. The role of Focus Housing Association, as a major provider, has also been instrumental in coordinated programme delivery. A strong community organisation, with Focus representatives alongside those from the City Council, and the Refugee Council, has also been effective in assisting the settlement process.

- Secondary migration is evident in the regrouping of Bosnians from other parts of the UK in Birmingham to overcome isolation by greater proximity to co-ethnics. These well-established processes have implications for RSL provision and the formation of RCOs where ethnic concentrations become more established.

General conclusions

This overview of specific community experiences reinforces many of the same lessons for RSLs, already documented by tenants in the previous chapter. Despite some positive evidence, community-based organisations and housing associations face an uphill struggle to establish their credentials and capabilities with the larger, more established RSLs and local authorities.

The key lessons for RSLs are:

- **RSLs can do much more to facilitate the role of communities and RCOs** and engage with them and the expertise they provide to deliver a comprehensive housing service. The resources from within the community groups offer a vital means of providing specialist support services.

- **Dispersal policies are not successful**, whereas the clustering of newly arrived refugees or asylum seekers offers better opportunities for RSLs and other agencies to coordinate provision and to develop support from within the community.

- **RSLs (and other providers) need to consider how the changing housing needs of this group can be best provided**. Different types of accommodation are required at different stages in the asylum seeker/refugee settlement cycle. The accommodation must also be responsive to the unique demographic and ethnic characteristics of the population.

- **Integrated provision of services**, in which housing and training are part of a coordinated settlement package, offer the best means of encouraging self-reliance in refugee communities.

- **Partnerships, drawing on the specialist resources and expertise of RCO partners, generate improved levels of tenant satisfaction** with the housing environment. RSLs should investigate ways of enhancing joint

working practices and partnerships in service provision.

- **Awareness of the specialist housing needs of local refugee communities**, as well as the opportunities which this provides for community-based RSLs to expand the range of housing they offer, can produce a successful outcome for both parties.

Generic issues for service providers

This section draws together generic findings from the case study locations, provides an overview of existing services and recommends improvements to services in the interests of users. The findings are aggregate account – size, location and objectives all have a bearing on the experiences of the RSLs and RCOs. However, there are a number of salient themes which need urgent remedial action if services to refugees and asylum seekers are to be sustained and improved. Our recommendations for action appear in Chapters 7 and 8. Although the analysis relates primarily to RSLs, the needs of RCOs and the significance of partnership between RCOs and RSLs are equally significant.

The period since the passing of the *1996 Asylum and Immigration Act* has been difficult for organisations dealing with refugees and asylum seekers. Wider structural and resource constraints remain fundamental barriers to strategic responses and the adoption of good practice. On the other hand, many of the concerns articulated by RCOs and their clients relate to problems rooted in poor working relationships between local authorities, RSLs and community groups. There is much scope for improving practice and further innovation.

- **In many RSLs there is a lack of explicit policies on refugees and asylum seekers**. Much of the practice appears crisis-driven in response to legislation and judicial rulings. Often services are delivered in a reactive and fragmented manner. The lack of a coherent strategic framework contributes to this problem, creating considerable uncertainty for both users and providers.

RSLs – power structures, partnerships and networks

- **One of the most significant barriers to more fruitful RCO/RSL relationships is the near monopoly of many local authorities over nominations.** Often, RSLs have little discretion to identify and pursue their own priorities for rehousing; RCOs have found themselves unable to negotiate partnerships with RSLs because of the reluctance of the local authority to relinquish their claims.

- **Financial constraints are compelling RSLs to be increasingly selective about their partners.** Internal audit work and risk analysis have produced tighter criteria for partnerships. Against the financial benefits, this process tends to exclude smaller groups, like RCOs – who may not have the necessary institutional capacity and organisational experience of larger more established groups – from access to RSL partnerships.

- **New initiatives in joint funding are driving both local authorities and RSLs to rationalise their partnerships with external organisations. This may exclude RCOs.** A more standardised approach to collaborative ventures with external agencies, through partnering and joint commissioning, is part of an overall trend in the public sector designed to achieve efficiency and value for money by streamlining the process of service delivery. The criteria used to select partners may exclude the smaller RCOs, which will often fall outside this inner circle. Rationalisation may stifle diversity and lead to a reduction in accountability.

- **There is little effective communication and networking between RSLs working with refugees and asylum seekers.** Although most local authorities operate liaison groups for associations working within their areas, there is little evidence of institutional learning or sharing of practice for asylum seeker and refugee provision.

- **This problem is compounded by a generally poor, and in some cases non-existent, dialogue between local authority housing departments and SSDs.**

- **Small and/or new RCOs experience considerable problems breaking into existing networks and tapping into 'power streams'.** There is a considerable degree of chance whether or not RCOs manage to get established. Success and failure depend less on performance and accountability and more about being in the right place at the right time which engenders powerlessness among many groups. The potential for patronage or nepotism that provides opportunities to some organisations which may not be equipped properly to deliver services, is a matter of concern.

- **Many RCOs are perceived less as partners and more like agents for the RSLs with whom they work.** This damages the potential development of smaller, community-based groups, restricting the diversity which is such an important characteristic of the voluntary sector.

- **RSLs are lax in their partnerships with RCOs.** Agency arrangements often lack clear provisions for assessing the needs of potential residents; extending long-term support for the RCO; and regulating performance standards. This is particularly the case with short life property. Significant improvements are needed in the mechanisms for monitoring performance, assessing the capacity of an RCO to deliver its commitments and measuring outcomes against original objectives.

RSLs – refugee and asylum seeker needs

- **There is a general lack of understanding of refugee and asylum issues among RSL staff.** Some households may have missed out on their potential entitlement as a result. Exceptions are mainly in RSLs which have developed closer working relationships with groups representing these households.

- **There is little effective service planning to meet the specialist needs of refugees and asylum seekers.** Many RSLs concentrate solely on the provision of accommodation to the exclusion of the support services for the needs of refugees and asylum seekers. This is an inadequate basis for future, sustainable services.

RCOs – barriers and opportunities

- **Many RCOs start out by managing short life property from local authorities or RSLs, an arrangement which is often perceived to work against them in the medium term.** By the time the properties have been upgraded and the community established, it is often time to hand the dwellings back. As a result, they receive little recognition for their efforts, nor are they able to generate any lasting assets. This has generated cynicism among many RCOs who feel they are being used as a cheap resource.

- **Some RCOs feel compelled to provide housing management services which may compromise other roles.** This is because alternative provision for their members does not exist or because they feel forced into performing the functions required by the association or local authority from which they lease dwellings. This may lead to role conflict and undermine their credibility. Effective advocacy and counselling can be compromised while RCOs are simultaneously engaged in management tasks, such as rent collecting and repairs, with their users.

- **RCOs managing housing contend that RSLs neglect the need for continuing support.** In many instances, this places a significant extra burden on the local community served by the RCO to provide additional support and resources to fill gaps.

- **Because of the wide diversity among RCOs, there are significant inconsistencies in standards of performance.** Some RCOs delivering poor levels of service are struggling to overcome major resource constraints. Only in a small number of cases does it appear that RCOs are lacking control, or that services deficiencies are so severe that fraud or complete failure would result. Unfortunately, the negative image of the few has tarnished the reputations of the better supported and structured organisations. RCOs and their tenants/clients often feel under greater scrutiny than might be the case for other groups.

- **There is little evidence of well-developed and effective networking between RCOs.** This is unusual in the voluntary sector where the need for coordination and cooperation is generally recognised as a high priority. This has created duplication and sometimes competition rather than collaboration, thereby reducing the potential for collective influence. Conversely, little or no additional resource could produce significant improvements to service delivery.

Funding

- **Access to funding and resources is a major issue for all organisations involved with refugees and asylum seekers.** RSLs may have the expertise to overcome some of the funding barriers, but this is rarely the case with smaller, specialist associations and RCOs who usually have neither the asset base to provide the security for capital loans nor the financial capacity to offer the level of innovation of the larger associations.

- **RSLs providing services to asylum seekers receive limited return on their investment.** The current situation is so uncertain that landlords have no idea how long a family in their property might wait for their application for asylum to be decided, or how the decision might go with consequential impacts on rent payment. Current trends indicate that only one in five cases are approved for full refugee status.

Training

- **There is a critical need for additional, specialist training for both RSL and RCO staff. Both sets of organisations have skills and knowledge deficiencies which significantly detract from their effectiveness and efficiency in providing services for refugees and asylum seekers.**

Conclusion

Housing provision and support services for refugees and asylum seekers in the public sector are patchy and inconsistent with no clear locational or organisational pattern. Organisations which might be expected to be the most appropriate providers of housing and support services – those located within the communities to be served – often underachieve.

RSLs providing housing to asylum seekers and refugees are operating under considerable resource constraints and the pressures of risk management. The majority of the RCOs exist on a shoe string and operate in a highly precarious financial state. As a result, deficiencies in training, the lack of well-developed networks and ineffective management systems characterise both RSLs and RCOs.

On the other hand, good practice and innovation exist and there is a considerable commitment among staff employed in these organisations; positive examples are detailed in Chapter 6. The fact that RCOs may have a very low profile should not prevent RSLs and other agencies from encouraging their development and full participation in the housing services offered. More recently arrived asylum seekers from countries where there are no pre-existing resident communities in the UK have substantial support needs.

Failure of RSLs to fully engage with RCOs is a structural problem, as much as one of organisational deficiency. To redress this shortfall, and to generate greater effectiveness and produce service improvements, a strategic approach is urgently required, involving all interested parties. This is detailed in the following chapters.

Good practice in housing management

Interpreting housing management

This chapter collates and documents examples of good practice in housing provision and services. Its focus is on housing performance for asylum seekers and refugees, rather than the overall qualities of an RSL. An initial concern was that uncertainty created by the *1996 Asylum and Immigration Act* and The Housing Corporation Circular (R3 – 04/97) might have resulted in a vacuum for refugees and asylum seeker services provided by RSLs. In practice, this has been less of a problem than anticipated. However, the legislation has had a negative effect by discouraging RSLs from offering housing services planned within a strategic framework. Good practice which does exist tends to be localised in a relatively small number of organisations.

In conducting the study, one challenge was how best to categorise practice to provide a useful framework for evaluation. But the diversity of organisations makes direct comparisons invidious and it is difficult and unfair to compare the performance of a small, unregistered RCO with a resource-rich RSL. Moreover, as the organisational typology in Chapter 3 illustrates, there is a balance of strengths and weaknesses between the generic and the specialist RSLs, which mark the best and worst landlords. Regardless of type, there are certain critical components determining the quality of service delivery to the user which have to be addressed whether managing one or 10,000 dwellings.

The approach adopted is to identify good practice within the organisations surveyed and then, in the section on good practice themes, to evaluate this practice against a series of criteria. The evaluation criteria reflect a balance between the specialist nature of the client group to be serviced, reasonable expectations of effectiveness, and value for money obligations placed on every organisation operating with or through public subsidy. The criteria are:

- access to housing and related services;
- innovative financing of projects;
- responsive and progressive management initiatives (including Housing Plus);
- means of supporting and empowering residents; and,
- the promotion and development of sustainable partnerships.

Each of these criteria has been at the forefront of recent trends in the development of good housing management practice. They represent a positive standard, or benchmark, against which to judge performance. Other practices fitted less neatly into these criteria; they were either unique to a location or interest group, or related more broadly to the approach and ethos of an organisation's activity. These have also been included where relevant.

The examples below illustrate the range and approach of RSLs in providing for refugees and asylum seekers. This is not a comprehensive list. A number of associations expected to be at the forefront of good practice chose not to participate in this study. Nor does the survey include every RSL nationally, which might house this client group. As much as possible, the examples reflect diversity and contrast. It is also important to recognise that this is a volatile environment with a changing pattern of responses and initiatives. This is a snapshot in time.

Examples of current good practice

Mainstream RSLs

Arawak/Walton Housing Association (AWHA). This is the largest black-led RSL in Manchester. It is an inner-city community-based association and 70% of the tenants are black British or black Afro-Caribbean. Having started life as Arawak in 1990, set up to meet the needs of the Afro-Caribbean community, it merged with Walton in 1994 and currently owns approximately 500 dwellings and manages a further 140 properties for other RSLs.

AWHA let 2% of tenancies to asylum seekers, and as these tenants attain full refugee status, AWHA designate other replacement properties for asylum seekers. It is committed, as an organisation, to rehousing and supporting refugees and asylum seekers within the objective of working with African and Caribbean households. This enables the RSL to develop significant levels of expertise and cultural awareness which may not be possible in more generic organisations.

> ### Arawak/Walton Housing Association – refugee policy
> - To promote Arawak Walton as an organisation which is proactive in respect of refugee housing through contact with community groups, family and friend connections with existing tenants, specialist organisations and representatives.
>
> - Positive discrimination in favour of refugees in the allocation of houses close to community networks and support provided that they also qualify in terms of housing need as defined in our lettings policy.
>
> - Commitment to work with and involve specialist community support organisations with specific skills and abilities related to the needs of refugees and other households recently entering the country.

> - Focusing our attention on refugee groups arriving from Africa and the Caribbean. Referring others to organisations with appropriate ethnic connections.
> - Working with support organisations and the individual household to ensure financial commitments are in place at the start of the tenancy to cover the cost of rent and other basic support needs.
> - To maintain contact and ensure social and welfare support remains in place during the early period of the tenancy or until the household no longer requires it.
> - To respond quickly to the housing needs of new refugee groups from Africa or the Caribbean as they arise, particularly those that have a connection with our existing community.

Source: Extracted from Arawak/Walton Annual Report 1997

Good practice
- Explicit commitment to the needs of refugees and asylum seekers elaborated in the association's policy statement which assists in communicating the message to staff and tenants.

- Express commitment by the board, in this statement, to new policy directions as a result of The Housing Corporation circulars.

East Thames Housing Group (ETHG). This operates in East London and parts of Essex and is the largest RSL in Newham. Although it does not record the number of refugees and asylum seekers in its stock, after the *1996 Housing Act*, up to a dozen lost their entitlement to benefit and were subsequently supported by SSDs under the *1948 National Assistance Act* or *1989 Children Act*.

ETHG has, in the past, developed partnerships with a number of smaller RSLs which include LABO, North London Muslim Housing Association, UJIMA, Home from Home, KUSH, Hibiscus and ASRA. In addition, it has also worked in partnership with the London Borough of Redbridge to set up and directly manage a small hostel.

Redbridge Project (Mayfair Road Hostel). The London Borough of Redbridge approached ETHG to help in providing for destitute single asylum seekers. The building was originally an old peoples' home, consisting of a six-bed property with shared facilities. It is close to the Redbridge Refugee Forum and the Borough's Community Advice Centre. An application was made to The Housing Corporation for the project to continue receiving Supported Housing Management Grant (SHMG).

The project houses six people and there is a contract between the local authority and ETHG, under which the SSD pays £130 (under the *1948 National Assistance Act*) per resident, which covers accommodation and food. This is reduced to a guaranteed £100 where a place is vacant. A project worker provides 17.5 hours support, mainly arranging for food delivery (residents cook their meals) and offering welfare advice. Food delivery has proved the most problematic aspect of the hostel. Redbridge Refugee Forum also offers assistance by providing information and translation services.

Virtually all ETHG's current activity with refugees and asylum seekers is now restricted to the Redbridge project, although it has provided direct financial support to Newham Refugee Centre to assist asylum seekers losing entitlement to housing.

Good practice
- Proactive in partnerships and networking with other providers and support services and organisations.
- Recognition of and sympathetic to negative impacts of legislative and judicial review changes, in relation to highly disadvantaged circumstances of asylum seekers.
- Provision of hostel accommodation and support services for destitute asylum seekers despite funding complexities – working round the constraints by providing alternative food source, etc.

English Churches Housing Association (ECHA). ECHA has been working with the London Borough of Lambeth to provide 130 bedspaces (70 for women, 60 for men) for single asylum seekers, in two local authority-owned ex-old

peoples' homes. With 24-hour housing management and two members of staff constantly on duty, ECHA aims to provide a safe and secure environment. In addition, in order to overcome the restrictions on asylum seekers receiving cash payments, it also provides three meals per day (which are delivered through external caterers), toiletries and travel passes. The housing workers liaise closely with the local SSD which funds the scheme through the eligible payments under the *1948 National Assistance Act*. Lambeth SSD provides support and translation where necessary, and the housing workers arrange for residents to sign up with local GPs, colleges, etc.

ECHA has also provided other units nationally, but these are dispersed within existing projects.

Good practice
- Range of creative initiatives to overcome funding constraints.
- Good liaison mechanisms with other organisations.
- Recognition of the need to provide high levels of continuous support and also management inputs.

Ealing Family Housing Association (EFHA). EFHA is a large RSL based in west London, Reading and Oxford. The Reading office has been part of an Emergency Provision Group which includes Reading Borough Council, the SSD and the voluntary sector, including Reading and Berkshire Refugee Support Group. Following the enactment of the *1996 Asylum and Immigration Act*, EFHA applied to the National Lottery for funds to employ a development worker. This was approved in October 1997 and resulted in a grant of £73,000 over three years.

The development worker also reports to a steering group which comprises members of the Emergency Provision Group, whose main brief is to create opportunities for refugees to find ways into work. This may be by training, education, work experience, and so on. The development worker assists refugees to utilise the range of skills to enhance their opportunity to achieve independence and enrich the quality of life.

Focus Housing Association. Since the 1940s one of the founding groups of Focus, COPEC, has assisted refugees in Britain. Twelve flats were made available to Polish refugees in the 1950s and 93 tenancies were given to the Vietnamese boat people in the 1970s. Five flats along with a community flat were given to people from the Bosnian community in 1992. At the present time Focus provides housing for approximately 135 refugees in 40 tenancies.

Focus has a policy of grouping refugee tenants in the same areas to aid the formation of community groups. When first providing tenancies, Focus deliberately locates refugees and asylum seekers within multi-cultural communities where, it is hoped, refugees can more easily assimilate and feel part of their surroundings. Focus' aim is to allow refugees to "stand on their own two feet", providing ongoing support to enable this to happen. As a practical example of this process, Focus has a furniture store to provide the basic requirements to move into unfurnished housing.

In addition to direct housing provision, Focus has also funded Shelter to provide specialist housing advisory staff. Focus does not employ its own in-house specialist workers, which might have been expected given their obvious commitment to housing refugees and asylum seekers. To do so might make a positive service even better.

Hexagon Housing Association. This is a medium-sized RSL based in South East London, managing 2,300 dwellings. It has worked with the London Borough of Bexley in the inception of a programme of 60 units to accommodate asylum seekers. Funded by a combination of local authority and Housing Corporation Social Housing Grant (SHG), the properties will all be family-sized street-level properties acquired on the open market. The dwellings will be let on assured shorthold tenancies which would be converted to shorthold tenancies should an asylum seeker be granted leave to remain. Hexagon charges slightly above the benchmark rent levels in order to fund a housing support worker for a six-month period to provide intensive housing management. However, this is still within the levels accepted as reasonable by the local authority. Additional support services will be supplied by the SSD with whom Hexagon has entered into a service level agreement. The RSL has also worked closely with voluntary sector support groups in order to provide additional services. Furniture will be provided which will be financed through a service charge.

Mosscare Housing Association. This is a community-based RSL in existence for over 25 years, based in Mosside in Manchester. It currently serves four local authority areas and manages 2,200 properties. Considerable institutional investment has been made to enable a community-based approach to its work, which has placed it in a good position to respond to specific community needs like asylum seekers and refugees.

It has developed lengthy experience with refugees starting with the Vietnamese in collaboration with Ockenden Venture. An example of its work with the community and the specific needs of refugees and asylum seekers is Mosscare's response in the Polish Elderly Refugees Project (see Chapter 5) developed in 1986, in collaboration with a local Roman Catholic Polish church, and which provides a full support network. The project comprises 50 new, SHG-funded flats, 25 of which were for Polish elders. Half of the nominations are through the Polish community and the other half are let to local authority nominees. There are currently two wardens, one of whom is Polish.

In late 1996 it started to accommodate asylum seekers in partnership with Manchester SSD and to a lesser extent Manchester Housing Department. This project is the subject of a formal agreement and accommodates 20 asylum seekers. Mosscare was approached by Manchester SSD which provides funding (under the eligible payments provision of the *1948 National Assistance Act* for single people 'without recourse to funds' and for families under the *1989 Children Act*) and welfare support. Mosscare provides accommodation and management services. There is a six-weekly review meeting cycle with all interested partners. There has been very limited turnover in the 20 or so asylum seeker tenancies referred by Manchester SSD. Mosscare does not provide specific refugee training for its two housing support and advice workers. However, they do receive general training and are responsible for new initiatives for all tenants.

In 1994 Mosscare instigated a policy of letting a number of furnished properties for new tenants. Although this predated the arrangement detailed above, the facility has proved useful for refugees and asylum seekers. Manchester SSD also initially provided starter packs for refugees and asylum seekers when the agreement first started. Now Mosscare has taken this on, with a commitment to a furniture budget recovered by rolling up the cost in the rent recovered over three or five years.

Mosscare is also in the process of developing a further new build scheme, in partnership with the Somali community and Manchester Housing Department for nominations. Mosscare already accommodates non-refugee Somalis and this new project will accommodate seven homeless households.

Mosscare has active links with Refugee Housing, providing office space, 10 units from their general stock and six short life dwellings which the Refugee Housing Association manage.

While refugees and asylum seekers have not been a general target group of the RSL, each of the projects described above fits well within its stated mission and attempts to provide services sensitive to the needs of refugees and asylum seekers.

Good practice

- Lengthy experience in providing housing for refugees which is fully endorsed at board level. This provides a positive message to front-line staff who feel confident in delivering effective services.
- Recognition of need for staged housing provision and specialist support, for example, native language speakers and national/ethnic compatibility of support workers. This is evident in an understanding of and response to specific refugee community needs.
- Creative initiatives with SSD for destitute asylum seekers with clearly worked-out partnership arrangements.
- Provision of training increases the potential responsiveness of the housing association to the specific needs of specialist tenants' groups like refugees and asylum seekers.
- Recognition of special needs of refugees and asylum seekers, for example, through furnished accommodation.
- Active involvement in partnership with RCO to build specifically for a refugee group and additional support for other RCOs (eg Refugee Housing).

Notting Hill Housing Trust (NHHT). NHHT accommodates over 100 asylum seekers at any given time. However, like virtually all other RSLs, it will not accept applicants who do not have the means of paying the rent. For asylum seekers, NHHT usually requires a letter from the SSD underwriting the rent. In addition, the association operates one scheme in partnership with the African Refugee Housing Association (ARHAG) comprising six self-contained flats.

NHHG also manages a scheme specifically for young single 16- to 18-year-old asylum seekers, won through competitive tender. The accommodation comprises eight large, leased houses with 27 bedrooms in Hillingdon. These have now been renovated to full Houses in Multiple Occupation (HMO) standards. The tenants share cooking and bathroom facilities but are encouraged in independent living. Some are able to claim housing benefit. Others receive assistance from SSDs to cover the costs. Each house is regularly visited and the association liaises directly with the SSD. The scheme receives no revenue support and is funded by rental income.

> **Good practice**
> * Development of partnerships with the local authority to provide specialist accommodation, that is, 16- to 18-year-olds. Associations often have the flexibility and expertise to provide the accommodation and services which reflect special needs.

Oxford Citizens Housing Association (OCHA).

The proximity to Campsfield House, the Home Office immigration detention centre in Kidlington, has produced a significant refugee community in the area. OCHA currently manages a nine-bedroom hostel and three-bedroom shared house for asylum seekers. OCHA also provides move-on facilities within its stock. Many of the asylum seeker clients are former detainees, as the Immigration Service recognises the project as providing suitable accommodation to which they might be released. OCHA has recruited a part-time specialist refugee worker who liaises with local voluntary organisations such as Asylum Welcome and Refugees in Oxford. In the medium to long run, OCHA are looking to work more closely with a specialist refugee agency.

> **Good practice**
> * Appointment of a specialist development worker, exclusively working with refugees, asylum seekers and related agencies.
> * Provision of move-on accommodation within permanent stock.

Providence Row Housing Association (PRHA).

Providence Row has a long history of provision for single homeless people from all backgrounds. It manages hostels with an aggregate bedspace of 300. With the exception of a 22 bedsits in the city, all of its hostels are located within Tower Hamlets. PRHA is one of the very few RSLs to incorporate asylum seekers in its mainstream hostels, rather than providing separate facilities. On average, this client group represents about 25% of residents in hostels (up to 50% in the 22 bedspace women-only hostel). These include refugees, asylum seekers with benefits and some who had lost benefits or who were referrals from local authorities.

The incorporation of asylum seekers in mainstream provision reflects the multi-cultural environment in Tower Hamlets and indicates the potential for the successful integration of asylum seekers into mainstream services. Such a model, in addition to facilitating successful integration, could reduce cost, risks, and the capital outlay involved in specialist service delivery.

PRHA's experience of mixing the two client groups has not created management problems (given that a high percentage of the BME population resides in the hostel) and to date this policy has not created financial problems. Refugees have different needs but, it is claimed, often need less intensive support compared with other residents.

PRHA also owns a hostel housing 80 residents. It is purpose-built and has won a design award. Unusually, it offers three different modes of accommodation: (a) room only, with no cooking facilities and with meals provided; (b) self-contained bedsits for those who need less support, preferred by those looking for part-time work and getting out of benefits (meals not included); and (c) flat-lets. There is also a special cluster for women, which has a 24-hour support service and regulation of visitors and visiting times. English language courses are provided in conjunction with a local college. PRHA's experience confirms that of St Mungo's (see below), that is, asylum seekers prefer to study languages in colleges, rather than on site, as this gives them an activity and stimulus outside the hostel. PRHA has also established a writing skills group, which helps asylum seekers to express their feelings about exile in a creative way.

PRHA organises cultural days in its hostels. This has involved inviting amateur and professional ethnic groups to perform in the hostel (in addition to the talents of refugee and refugee residents). These events have proved extremely successful in providing entertainment; boosting the self-esteem of residents; creating a social/non-formal atmosphere for management and residents and for various ethnic groups within the locality to know each other and exchange ideas. The events also helped to break down the barriers between the hostel and the local community as community groups from outside the hostel were encouraged to attend. The settlement officer has fundraised for these events, which run twice a year. PRHA encourages residents to attend the hostel's staff 'getting involved meetings'. All agenda items are open for discussion; there are no separate meetings for staff and clients. The intention is to encourage residents to 'own' their settlement process. However, only a very small percentage of residents usually attend, and asylum seekers are generally not represented.

Good practice
- Extensive multi-cultural experience and willingness to experiment with different forms of accommodation tailored to different needs of groups of asylum seekers and refugees.
- Sensitivity to the resettlement needs of refugees and asylum seekers, for example, the provision of language and writing classes.
- Provision of a variety of activities and group participation strategies to integrate tenants and staff and to develop self-esteem of asylum seekers.
- Engaging with local community groups to break down the barriers between the hostel residents and the local community; tension

between the two groups is frequently a problem where refugees and asylum seekers are housed in relatively large groups.
- Facilitating empowerment, through social activities and participation in meetings, to encourage residents to 'own' their settlement process.

St Mungo's Housing Association (SMHA). St Mungo's experience in providing (exclusively) for asylum seekers started with a 20-bedspace hostel in Harrow Road, West London. This, combined with the association's history in dealing with homelessness for single adults, encouraged St Mungo's to offer their services when the London Borough of Lambeth requested assistance in providing for single asylum seekers. In November 1997, the SSD identified an empty, 61-bedspace old persons' hostel in SW9, and the building was quickly refurbished and furnished. As a purpose-built hostel, the property offers many facilities and space for recreation and hobbies, cooking and dining, training and so on.

Staff members are in daily contact with the residents. Residents do not receive benefits. Staff at the hostel have been innovative in developing a range of schemes designed to alleviate, where possible, the financial difficulties experienced by residents. For example, it has recruited a volunteer to fundraise for a hardship fund to provide residents with resources for essential items such as clothing and shoes. It has organised day trips and developed special rate admission arrangement with local cinemas and sport centres. PCs have been borrowed to help students and those interested in IT. SMHA also supports an art studio for residents interested in painting as therapy for torture victims. A volunteer psychiatrist has provided in-house regular surgeries; this has led to the development of a referral procedure to the Medical Foundation for Victims of Torture.

Although there are monthly hostel meetings and resident committees, residents have shown little interest in attending. As an alternative, a questionnaire was developed to identify needs and the response was encouraging. Among the issues identified by residents was the need for up-to-date information regarding asylum procedures and changes in benefits. Consequently, information gathering and dissemination mechanisms within the hostel were improved.

Good practice
- SMHA has built on its extensive experience to provide tailor-made accommodation and, especially, a range of support services which are sensitive to the needs of refugees and asylum seekers.
- There is an extensive and innovative range of social activities, training programmes, financial support for essential items, therapy and psychiatric support for asylum seekers. The scope and approach are commended to other RSLs.
- It has experimented with different methods of encouraging tenant participation.

Springboard Housing Association (SHA). SHA has a history of providing accommodation for refugees and asylum seekers from Ugandan Asians in the 1970s, and South Africans exiled during the apartheid regime. More recently, during the Bosnian crisis in 1997, SHA worked with Essex County Council to provide temporary shelter for over 100 Muslims from Kosovo. Springboard ultimately provided permanent housing for four households who were unable to make alternative arrangements.

SHA is now networking with local authorities in whose areas they work, and has indicated their interest in housing refugees and asylum seekers. Each local authority will be able to nominate a maximum of three households, with a total ceiling of 21.

SHA also has partnerships with the Refugee Housing Association (RHA), leasing property for three years, and an agreement with Karin Housing Association (a Somali housing association based in Tower Hamlets) to manage one property.

Good practice
- Strategic approach to the provision of housing for refugees and asylum seekers. Clear indications given to local authorities of the involvement of the association. This

will enable better planning and the creation of more sustainable services.
- Partnership between mainstream RSL and smaller associations and RCOs. This makes the best use of resources and provides encouragement and support for smaller organisations to develop further.

Wandle Housing Association (WHA). WHA is a London-based RSL which currently owns three schemes let to refugees. WHA works with the London Borough of Wandsworth to allocate short-term and permanent housing to refugees nominated through the local authority. The day-to-day management is undertaken by Refugee Housing who collect the rent, provide support and carry out routine repairs. WHA is responsible for capital repairs and receives an income by claiming Transitional Special Needs Management Allowance (TSNMA).

One of the schemes offers nine first-stage bedspaces. These are for refugees who need a higher level of support before moving on into independent accommodation. Two other schemes, one with seven female bedspaces, the other with seven male bedspaces, offer second-stage accommodation. In some instances, WHA offers final-stage accommodation in independent, permanent housing.

Good practice
- Partnership between both local authority and specialist RSL.
- Use of flexible, staged accommodation linked to permanent, move-on housing. This recognises the changing housing needs of refugees and asylum seekers at different stages of the resettlement process.
- Use of TSNMA to ensure viability of properties.

Refugee Housing Association (RHA)

RHA started in the mid-1950s when British Council for Aid to Refugees Housing Society Ltd was formed to help Hungarian refugees. In 1994 RHA joined with the housing division of the

Refugee Council to establish the present Refugee Housing Association. In March 1997, RHA merged with Metropolitan Housing Trust (MHT) and is now part of this larger organisation.

Table 4: Number of units/bedspaces owned and managed

Rehabilitated units	241
Non-rehabilitated	193
Private sector leases	61
Managed for other housing associations	33
New build	31
Total	**559**
Hostels	
Private sector lease hostels bedspaces	99
Owned hostel bedspaces	46
Managed for other housing association hostel/bedspaces	335
Total	**480**

Currently, RHA own or manage over 1,000 bedspaces dispersed around the UK. The organisation is rationalising its stock in order to concentrate within a smaller number of defined geographical areas where refugee and asylum seeker needs are most concentrated.

RHA specialises in provision for port applicants (entitled to benefits) and its approach is to facilitate settlement by empowering tenants to attain independent living in the community. An asylum seeker accepted as an RHA tenant might go through three stages of accommodation: initial reception, second-stage hostels and access into a permanent dwelling. This structured support is especially valuable for people who have no obvious community support on which to rely. The main referral agency is the Refugee Arrivals Project (RAP), although they receive nominations from other government-funded bodies, the Refugee Council and some RCOs.

RHA manages three reception centres and the majority of clients are young single people (23-35 years), 60% male and 40% female. The admission criteria are based on an assessment of the degree of vulnerability and the specific support necessary to meet the needs identified during the assessment process. In general, residents do not stay in reception centres for more than 12 months, but this ultimately depends on the vulnerability of the individual client. Residents are encouraged to seek support and extend links with the refugee community and voluntary organisations. The centres provide 24-hour support with a key worker system.

The reception centres are funded by rent, Supported Housing Management Grant (SHMG) (three-year) and support from the London Boroughs Grant Unit (LBGU) (annually).

The second-stage hostels provide less intensive care, with a lower ratio of support worker to residents. Full 24-hour cover is not provided. The main emphasis is on developing skills for independent living in the community. The majority of second-stage hostels are managed by the RHA on behalf of other partner housing associations. The sources of finance are similar to the reception centres.

RHA has also been assigned the role of clearing house for the HOMES Refugee quota. Currently 24 agencies participate in the project which provides for non-priority homeless people to be rehoused. Under the scheme, a quota is allocated to refugee agencies of which 75% is nominated from short reception or hostel schemes.

Refugee community groups

Tamil Housing Association: the Tamil Refugee Action Group (TRAG) was established in 1985. It was soon realised that to fulfil the housing need of refugees, TRAG would have to develop a specialised arm and the Tamil Refugee (Action Group) Housing Association was formed in January 1986. In 1990 TR(AG)HA became TRHA. Attempts to register as a full housing association with The Housing Corporation have, to date, been unsuccessful. TRHA has the status of a management agency (semi-registered status).

TRHA is a management agency for properties provided by large RSLs with 224 short life bedspaces and 74 permanent units. Permanent stock is developed by obtaining capital funding from The Housing Corporation in partnership with larger RSLs. Partners include various local authorities and RSLs including London &

Quadrant, Metropolitan, Hyde and Family Housing Associations.

TRHA has also received grants from The Housing Corporation for research and training purposes (Promotional and Advisory Grant) and Special Need Management Allowances (SNMAs) for managing hostels for men and women.

The Association has its own waiting list and receives referrals from Tamil organisations, RAP, other refugee community organisations, local authorities, social services and local hospitals. Ninety per cent of tenants are Tamils and the rest are refugee and asylum seekers from other countries. Of these, 90% of tenants are asylum seekers and 10% have full refugee status. Eighty per cent of tenants are dependant on welfare assistance to pay their rent.

LABO: this is a predominantly Bangladeshi housing association which evolved from a housing community project (Lime Housing Project, established 1984) aimed at combating local homeless among the community. LABO was registered in 1989 and the majority of its stock is in Tower Hamlets, but more recently it has started developing in Newham. A major objective has been to address the problem experienced by large families in the community who were increasingly housed outside the borough because of a shortage of suitably sized accommodation. Accordingly, LABO provides local large family dwellings wherever possible, and this remains a distinct characteristic of LABO's housing stock, that is, houses of between three to five bedrooms.

Presently, LABO has 146 units (of which 10 only are short life) and it is currently developing 40 units. The total number of people housed is 650. The majority of tenants are Bangladeshis (50%) and about 15% are Somalis. The two communities share the same religion and some demographic characteristics, such as large families. The number of refugee and asylum seekers is not monitored but many of the Somali tenants are refugees. Many are female-headed households who have lost their husbands in wars, and are in need of high levels of support. Support for this group is described as one of the main aims of the Association.

LABO has worked in partnership with a range of mainstream RSLs, including East Thames Housing Group, Peabody Trust and Bethnal Green and Victoria Park Housing Association, all of which have offered development services. More recently, LABO has begun to initiate its own developments. This will enable the Association to give greater priority and care to certain aspects of ethnic minority living (storage space, washing facilities, kitchen design etc), for which other developers tend to be less sensitive. LABO also works in collaboration with other housing associations which include ARHAG and Karin Housing Association.

A key component of LABO's core activities is to work closely with community organisations (Bangladeshi, Somali and Chinese Community groups as well as an ethnic mental health organisation) and to arrange referral agreements where appropriate.

A tenant forum was established in 1995 and LABO has been active in areas more recently recognised as Housing Plus. It has provided training in office work (working as volunteers) for tenants and is currently considering developing a credit union. It has recently developed a video, *Houses and homes – A guide to looking after your home* using an Innovation and Good Practice Grant (IGP). The video is "designed to help assist residents in looking after their properties offering practical advice and tips to deal with issues such as condensation, heating, rubbish disposal and care for common areas". LABO believes that the video was well received and helped considerably in reducing call outs. It is available in English, Urdu, Bengali, Somali, Punjabi and Cantonese.

Good practice themes

Having examined a significant amount of practice across a range of RSLs and RCOs, some aspects of the practice identified above are largely underdeveloped, in particular, empowerment and financial innovation. Others, such as partnership and management support, are more widespread, although Housing Plus initiatives are less evident. Access and the processes leading to an offer are poorly developed areas of practice. These generated more negative comments.

Overall, as noted in Chapter 4, asylum seekers and refugees are generally satisfied in their contact with associations. This confirms a study of the housing needs of refugees in the north of England carried out by HACT (HACT, 1994a) which indicated that 51% of the refugees interviewed had dealt with housing associations. The majority found them helpful, especially in relation to the speed of offer, quality of property and service and maintenance.

Yet, as indicated in Chapter 5, there is considerable variation in the quality of practice, much of which, if not overtly bad, is certainly mediocre. It is important to stress again that part of the explanation of poor practice lies in the structural constraints – government policies and legislation, reductions in public expenditure in this sector. But it also arises from organisational inefficiency, limited institutional capacity, and/or ineffective policies and practices borne out of inadequate training, knowledge or resources. Many of the reasons which lie behind these shortfalls in practice have been identified in Chapter 5 and are addressed further in Chapter 7.

Access

This aspect of service delivery has often caused the greatest level of concern and dissatisfaction. It is singled out by the refugees and asylum seekers interviewed (Chapter 4); but is also reflected by RCOs. A major part of the problem, as identified in earlier chapters, is the shortage of available accommodation, particularly in the South. This has meant that non-statutory applicants often stand little chance of obtaining social housing.

Asylum seekers and their advocates perceive that many of the larger non-specialist associations lack appreciation of the different and specific needs of refugees and asylum seekers. Many have suffered post-traumatic stress disorder arising from their experiences of incarceration, torture, constant surveillance and/or oppression and harassment. This makes shared or communal living a much more problematic experience than for the majority of domestic single homeless cases. Yet few service providers are aware of or have taken account of the psychological needs of asylum seekers in service planning and delivery. The pressures for cost reduction result in the creation of quite inappropriate environments. For example, some

housing providers are using dormitories or small shared rooms to accommodate people who are complete strangers, which could have disastrous implications. The real effects of these practices might not be immediately visible to service providers as many asylum seekers, rather than complaining, have opted to leave such accommodation to sleep on a friend's floor.

The organisations which have the most effective mechanisms for identifying need among refugees and asylum seekers are RCOs which are firmly rooted in the community. Paradoxically, because of many of the constraints identified in the last chapter, they are least able to offer the dwellings needed.

It is important that RSLs in general make themselves aware of the full extent of the needs of refugees and asylum seekers and operate access policies which are sensitive and responsive to these needs.

Finance

Financial constraints lie at the root of the majority of problems experienced by RSLs and RCOs. The former find it difficult to raise finances because they have few assets and are not usually registered with The Housing Corporation. The mainstream RSLs can, in normal circumstances, only access funds via commercial loans which have to be repaid. But this means minimising financial risks, and asylum seekers in particular, because of disentitlement since 1996, tend to be the least secure risk as a tenant group. Even if they receive support from SSDs, the uncertainty surrounding applications for asylum makes RSLs reluctant to offer what might be short-term tenancies.

Thus, rather than supporting destitute or impoverished asylum seekers, the vast majority of RSLs have taken an inflexible view, choosing not to accept asylum seekers without the means to pay the rent. In only a handful of instances have RSLs absorbed unrecoverable rental payments from asylum seekers. For existing tenants, however, some of the larger RSLs have set up hardship funds to cover cases where benefit entitlement might be curtailed. These funds have been used very infrequently.

The main area of financial innovation involves RSLs developing short-term provision – usually hostel accommodation – using an income stream guaranteed by SSDs as payments under the *1948 National Assistance Act*. There are several variations on this theme. Generally, they involve an RSL identifying a suitable building, usually fairly large so as to generate economies of scale, and providing support, meals (or vouchers), toiletries and travel vouchers.

Most of the innovative approaches were small scale, for example, where RSLs such as Mosscare and Arawak/Walton have used funds to provide refugees and asylum seekers with the basic essentials to move into a new home. By recycling funds, the cost to the RSL is minimal, but the benefit to the new tenant is significant. Associations often have considerable capacity to use their finances more creatively, at no risk to themselves, and at little or no cost. This potential should be investigated wherever possible.

Management

Housing management is a critical area of concern for both service deliverers and consumers. There is wide variation in approaches to and quality of housing management delivered to asylum seekers. The management style of the organisation is a major determinant of quality which, in the best examples, blends high quality basic housing management with sensitive levels of support and personal development to ensure effective resettlement. All too often, however, the quality focus is skewed towards one of these areas at the expense of the other.

In general, management practice is more effective in black-led and refugee-specific organisations. This derives from either greater empathy with the client group, or innovative and experimental approaches to delivering housing management. These were both areas identified in previous research into the role of BME associations delivering value-added services (West and Lemos, 1996). The report, *Flair in the community*, contended that "the most contingent benefit is that black associations, more so than almost any other social housing provider, involve the community that is being served in the running of the association" (West and Lemos, 1996). This factor is equally of crucial importance for refugees and asylum seekers who are usually highly dependent on the local community for support and assistance. Black-led RCOs and RSLs are particularly strong in this way of working.

Organisations such as LABO, Tamil Housing Association and Refugee Housing Association have a cultural attachment to the Housing Plus concept of housing management. This locates tenants at the heart of service delivery, and contrasts with RSLs geared more towards an asset-focused service. But this approach is also evident in more generic associations such as Notting Hill Housing Trust, Focus and Mosscare. The difference is mainly in strength of focus. In the case of the BME organisations, their links and expertise are limited to relatively few client groups and their empathy is translated into services with greater effect. The generic associations, on the other hand, cater for a much broader range of needs and adopt a more uniform approach to service delivery. This does not necessarily diminish their effectiveness, but can limit the extent to which they can tailor support for several specific groups.

Empathy is not the sole determinant of service quality. Its value can easily be diminished by poor resource management – the cornerstone of any viable housing organisation in the current political and financial climate. The best organisations are those which most effectively combined the two, producing high quality management within a sensitive and responsive framework. Many fell short of this target.

Empowerment

There is a noticeable lack of good practice in this area. Evidence of concern and good intentions to empower this group are not borne out by strategies which, more often than not, fail to take the special circumstances of the client group into account. Many providers have put the issue of empowerment in the background, concentrating their efforts on providing basic services.

Asylum seekers, especially those without benefits, are among the most vulnerable groups that social landlords have to deal with. As a result, asylum seekers tend not to assert their tenancy rights, particularly in terms of lodging complaints or requesting additional services. Many will have lived in countries where the institutional or political environments discourage dissent and do not value its potentially positive contribution. Almost by definition, dissidence, or raising one's voice, are associated with harsh treatment, personal trauma and the process of asylum seeking. One asylum seeker we interviewed illustrates this point very well. She is a 29-year-old Ethiopian living in a hostel for destitute asylum seekers. She had moved her bedclothes on to the floor and no longer slept in her bed. When questioned about this, she explained that the room was draughty and she had been cold for sometime. Although she had asked for the window to be repaired at the onset of winter, nothing had been done and she did not wish to cause trouble by asking again: "complaining too much is why I had to leave my country. If they don't want to fix the window I avoid it by sleeping on the floor, no problem!" Another reason for reluctance to participate is the perception that one is a 'passing guest' and as such should not be too difficult for one's hosts. A refugee who worked as a coordinator of a large refugee organisation revealed that in a similar situation he always reflected, "remember, you are only a stranger in this country, you should be grateful that they saved your life".

A further barrier to active tenant involvement is the concern about the impact of complaints on the determination of the claim for asylum. Many asylum seekers are convinced that "making trouble" will negatively affect their chances. Many asylum seekers appear to go to great lengths to avoid asking for their entitlements or challenging a decision, believing that causing less trouble, or not asking for badly needed support, would prove the authenticity of their case. Dispelling any suggestion that they are economic refugees, drawn to the UK by its state handouts, they are convinced, improves their chances of remaining in the country.

Even those who possess the communication skills or the will to pursue a complaint might not have the knowledge of the necessary procedures. However, the majority of social landlords issued tenants clear guidelines on complaints and provided additional support such as translated versions or interpretation

of documents. Notice boards were also used to reinforce the message. In some cases, hostel workers had encouraged 'buddying' or mentoring arrangements: established residents were paired with newer and/or more vulnerable residents to offer informal advice and support. This is reassuringly good practice even if the opportunities are not taken up. However, there are cases where tenants are either not aware of their rights or believe that they had insufficient power to challenge the system.

Many refugees and asylum seekers have an enormous amount to offer their landlords. They are usually well qualified and have been in positions of significant responsibility and/or influence in their country of origin. It is important that they have the opportunity to become involved, to develop a sense of worth and potentially offer hugely beneficial assistance to RSLs.

Most of the organisations studied were committed to involving their tenants in some level of participation. However, there is little evidence of this commitment being translated into effective service delivery for refugees and asylum seekers. Greater recognition is needed among RSLs, in particular, of the significant potential within this client group and the benefits of using their skills and knowledge. This can only be achieved with greater understanding of the complex barriers (both cultural and institutional) which prevent fuller participation from taking place, coupled with improved training for both staff and tenants on how to work together.

Partnerships

Identifying effective partnership mechanisms was anticipated to be one of the principal findings of the study. There are many parties involved in the support and housing of refugees and asylum seekers, and the voluntary sector has a track record of successful collaboration. However, contrary to this assumption, partnership is an area which requires substantial improvement.

This is not to suggest that examples of good practice do not exist. A number of organisations have worked successfully with and through other agencies: good examples are LABO, Refugee Housing Association and Notting Hill Housing Trust, which have developed relationships with their partners which go further than purely financial objectives. In contrast, there is worrying reluctance by quite a number of RSLs and RCOs to engage in constructive dialogue or share a perceived advantage.

This, in part, indicates the need for additional training, particularly for staff working in small, specialist organisations. However, it also highlights an increasing element of competition affecting some organisations and reducing the degree to which they are prepared to operate in an open and flexible manner. To some extent, this is understandable, with too many organisations chasing too few resources; but this trend can only work to the disadvantage of service users.

Hostels

Current trends in provision and increasing demand emphasise the importance of diversity in the range of housing and support for refugees and asylum seekers. However, diversity can sometimes mean fragmentation and under-resourcing, to the detriment of service users. Diversity is needed, but within a framework which recognises the different stages of resettlement and the different housing needs at each stage.

A key concern expressed by those involved in this area is the need for a coordinated strategy of reception and initial resettlement. Perhaps because innovative examples are lacking, hostels are currently the main form of provision for this initial stage, a topic already touched on in Chapter 3. They seem to offer a balance between cost and

effectiveness. Hostel provision is also an area of housing practice which offers a practical opportunity to deliver good practice themes listed above. Hostel provision is, of course, identified in the government's review of asylum policy, as the major feature of proposals designed to manage and control public expenditure on asylum seekers.

In this section the different models of hostel provision are examined, together with their potential role in a network of good practice for refugees and asylum seekers.

Many local authorities and RSLs interviewed in London agree that hostels managed by RSLs would provide the most effective way of housing destitute asylum seekers. However, in practice, the quality of hostel accommodation provision varies considerably between local authorities. In the shadow of the anticipated government review of asylum policy, local authorities have been uncertain about how long they would be expected to shoulder responsibility for this client group. This has been a major discouragement to them and other service providers, and has made it difficult to plan and deliver viable services under a constantly changing body of case law.

An example of service blight is in the London Borough of Camden, where the authority contacted a number of RSLs to assist in developing and managing hostels. Notting Hill Housing Trust offered the preferred package of accommodation and services, but wished to enter into a three-year contract. Camden considered it "not feasible for the authority to enter into contracts for longer than 12 months pending the outcome of the Home Office inquiry which is going to determine the ultimate responsibility for asylum seekers" (London Borough of Camden: Asylum Seekers Update, 4/2/1998, p 4). Many potentially positive and innovative proposals have foundered on such uncertainty.

Model 1: Local authority sponsored, RSL managed
This alternative allows an equitable sharing of the risks outlined above. Local authorities have provided empty buildings requiring no major adaptation, but which could be used for other purposes if and when they are no longer responsible for asylum seekers. An RSL would then be invited to lease the property and refurbish it with the assistance of SHG. In many cases a contribution from the authority has been required and a peppercorn rent has been charged to reduce scheme costs to a minimum.

Example: St Michael's Church Hall, Greenland Road, NW1 (Bridge Housing Association/London Borough of Camden)

A Church hall in Camden town was originally developed by Camden Temporary Housing Group in partnership with Bridge Housing Association and St Michael's Church, as a winter shelter of 35 units of shared accommodation, using a DETR grant. A subsequent proposal was later agreed by the local authority to use the property as a supported housing scheme for asylum families (maximum 28 persons). It was approved to house 10 individual family units of up to four persons with common space in the form of a dining room, TV rooms and kitchens. Bridge Housing Association, who ran the Winter Shelter, were appointed to manage the project.

Good practice issues: partnership between the statutory, RSL and voluntary sectors; creative use of existing resources.

These partnerships have worked best when local authorities are committed to providing asylum seeker housing within their authority area. Examples of success include the London Borough of Lambeth in partnership with St Mungo's Housing Association, the London Borough of Islington (in partnership with Providence Row Housing Association), London Borough of Barking and Dagenham (East Thames Housing Association), and the London Borough of Camden (Bridge Housing Association).

Model 2: Local authority owned and managed hostels

In this model, local authorities establish and run their own hostels in order to minimise the cost. This model is outside the study remit and has not been examined in depth. Anecdotal evidence suggests that these schemes cater for large numbers with fewer care elements provided.

Model 3: Voluntary sector hostels

In this model, smaller RSLs or RCOs develop and operate hostel accommodation at the smaller end of the scale. An example is the Cedar Project (Asylum Seekers Children) in Uxbridge, housing 10, under-18-year-old asylum seekers. It provides intensive care and support in close collaboration with the London Borough of Hillingdon SSD.

Typically, voluntary sector hostels average less than 10-12 units and quality varies substantially between organisations. The small size reduces scale economies which may lead to perhaps weaker housing management. Conversely the small size enables intensive support services to be provided which are considered so important. The small scale often means that there are insufficient resources to staff and train workers adequately to undertake the routine management functions.

Model 4: Private sector

Examples

Hostel at Leabridge Road, Waltham Forest. This a hostel for 112 single asylum seekers run by a private company (Elitelodge Ltd), charging rent of £139 per week, and when fully occupied generates an income of over £800,000 pa. There is quite a high staff level to reassure the local community.

King's Cross Hostel, run by Gulliver Projects Ltd, provides a 43-bed hostel comprising 10 single rooms (£97.20 per week per room), 10 doubles (at £169.20) and 1 triple (at £234.90 per week per room). The total income which could potentially be generated is over £200,000 pa. Rental charges include breakfast and the Asylum Team provides residents with a food voucher of £21 per person per week. The staffing complement is two workers by day and one by night. Staff are required to inform the council of any problems and changes in the tenants' circumstances. Tenants have to sign a register and staff have to report any tenant who has not been seen for 24 hours.

Source: London Borough of Camden, Report to Social Services Committee, 4 February 1998

Following the High Court ruling in October 1977 SSDs in London were inundated by approaches from private companies offering full board accommodation or meal services. These were predominantly outside London (eg Eastbourne, Leicester and Cleethorpes) in locations where costs were significantly lower than in the capital. Not surprisingly, such companies, like their RSL counterparts, were also anxious to enter into contracts for longer than 12 months and/or secure block contracts. Private provision usually comprises a very low-level package of care elements and so the comparative cheapness is largely due to a combination of reduced service levels and large numbers.

In support of this option, despite the obvious disadvantages, many of the RCOs interviewed felt that placing asylum seekers out of London compromises their well-being by depriving them of the essential services and community support generally concentrated in London (community support, legal support from immigration specialists etc). It has also been argued, on the other hand, that some local authorities are using out-of-London services as a deterrent to reduce the flow of asylum seekers. (There was a drop in the number of asylum seekers approaching the London Borough of Newham immediately after they opted to use the Eastbourne Hostel, which was subsequently outlawed on appeal.)

Ironically, housing asylum seekers currently appear to be commercially viable for the private sector. The indications are that private landlords now prefer accommodating destitute asylum seekers rather than housing benefit claimants, because SSD payment is made direct to landlords. This is far less complicated and risky than relying on housing benefit. Both the Refugees Arrival Project (RAP) and the Refugee Council currently report that, within the private sector, it is easier to find accommodation for destitute asylum seekers than for those with benefits.

Model 5: The Consortium approach

In an attempt to find a strategic solution to the asylum crisis, the London Borough of Westminster led a number of London boroughs (Kensington & Chelsea, Hammersmith, Lambeth, Camden, and Newham) in an examination of ways to share expertise, costs, etc, and to promote sustainable solutions. The Consortium has pursued a number of options, usually involving rehousing asylum seekers in large hostels, and has involved government departments in its proposals to ensure that immigration and welfare services are provided on site.

One potential approach on these lines is the orthodox European model of reception centres to which all new arrivals are referred initially for processing asylum claims. This is then followed by subsequent relocation as each individual case is dealt with. To a certain extent this is the model envisaged in the government's proposed review. Many of the RSLs interviewed expressed a cautious welcome about their possible involvement in managing reception centres. The main concern related to issues of security and freedom of movement of residents. The Consortium envisages a major role for RSLs working alongside active voluntary organisations, if the proposals are enacted.

Rent Guarantee/Deposit Schemes

As it becomes increasingly difficult for refugees and asylum seekers to access social housing, the private rented sector is the only alternative open for this client group in many areas. Yet, evidence from our RCO focus groups and other voluntary providers shows that it is also becoming increasingly difficult for refugees and asylum seekers to access this sector too. Letting agencies are finding it difficult to recruit landlords willing to accept SSD tenants or those unable to provide deposit and/or acceptable references. Uncertainty and confusion regarding rights of refugees and asylum seekers add to this difficulty. Consequently, many refugees and asylum seekers, in particular, single asylum seekers in London, are finding it equally difficult to access the private housing sector. Rent-in-Advance Guarantee/Deposit Schemes (RAGDS), which come in variety of forms, have the potential of helping refugees and their carers in accessing the private housing sector. Recognising the scale of the problem and the potential role of RAGDS in reducing management problems and financial risks, the Refugee Council, in partnership with RAP and RHA, worked to develop a RAGDS. The London Borough of Lewisham's Private Sector Housing Unit provided active support for the project, together with other agencies, such as local letting agencies and RSLs.

This pilot scheme could serve as a model for wider use. It is based on the following elements:

- a scheme fund from which four weeks rent in advance is paid to a participating landlord and recouped through housing benefit; subsequent rent payments go directly to the landlord/management agent;

- instead of a cash deposit, a written guarantee is issued against an agreed inventory, any subsequent liability being met by the scheme fund within agreed limits;

- potential tenants are referred by participating agencies and the suitability of each referral is assessed prior to acceptance on to a waiting list;

- properties and landlords are vetted and the scheme acts as an 'honest broker' between the two parties;

- the scheme provides advice and practical support to landlords and tenants in areas such as housing benefit services, tenancy agreements, property standard, language/communication, etc.

Follow-up/resettlement support has been found to be crucial in the pilot scheme, on financial as well as welfare grounds. This has helped to reduce the considerable management problems which landlords and agents experienced with "housing benefit claimants which was exacerbated when dealing with asylum seekers/refugees who had language difficulties or were unfamiliar with the welfare benefit system and tenancy responsibilities" (Refugee Council).

There are at least two reasons for commending RSL involvement in the development of these schemes. The first is particularly pertinent to RSLs which provide supported housing for asylum seekers, many of whom experience difficulty in finding adequate move-on facilities in the social housing sector. The use of RAGDS might be a cost-effective way of generating additional options to supplement and revive the flagging move-on process. However, as the project report notes, the adoption of RAGDS is not at all straightforward. Organisations have an uphill struggle to overcome the expectations of hostel residents who are often set on moving into permanent social housing. There is also the cultural inertia of the organisations themselves, particularly among those used to working exclusively within the social housing sector.

Second, the development of RAGDS also provides scope for action where RSLs are unable to offer direct provision, for example, because of tight local authority control over nomination agreements. Either independently or in partnership with other providers (eg RCOs), RSLs could develop RAGDS as a way of facilitating access to private housing for clients who seek access to housing directly through them or their RCO partners. RSLs could provide services such as inspection of properties, training for support workers, legislative and management advice, and help in establishing contacts with private landlords and local authority officers.

A number of agencies offer generalist RAGDS which are increasingly used by refugees and asylum seekers. These include East London Home Link,

Oxford Citizens Housing Trust and Brighton Housing Trust. Of the 17 referral agencies involved in the Refugee Council's pilot project there were five RSLs: Beaver Housing Society – 'Letting Plus' Project; Central and Cecil Housing Trust – Waterloo Road Hostel; Riverpoint – Manor Place Hostel; The Providence Housing Project; Refugee Housing Association.

Safelet scheme

Another project, developed for destitute asylum seekers, is the Safelet project. This scheme was developed as a partnership between Bailey Housing Association and Bexley Council and is used by the local authority to discharge its duties under the *1948 National Assistance Act*.

The Safelet scheme was launched in April 1996, in anticipation of the *1996 Housing Act*, restricting benefits and access to social housing. Bailey Housing Association administers the scheme with the assistance of the housing advisory service of the London Borough of Bexley. The scheme works closely with two other agents: the Borough SSD's Refugee and New Arrivals Coordinator (RNAC) and the Bexley Churches Homelessness Project. The latter provides the funds for a Deposit and Rent in Advance Service (RADGS), which is used to compensate participating landlords for any damage caused to their properties.

The scheme works as an accommodation agency, offering support and advice to both tenants (who, in the main, are single homeless people) and landlords. Safelet recruits landlords, advises them on all aspects of renting, and matches the accommodation that becomes available to suitable tenants. All asylum seeker referrals to the scheme are made in the first instance to the housing department. Applicants who are assessed as people from abroad from an 'excluded class' are referred to the Social Service's RNAC. Single asylum seekers for whom the SSD has a legal duty are then referred to Safelet through a standard form which provides personal details of the client, client's language, entitlement to benefits, details of the client's solicitor and date when client's application for refugee status is to be considered by the Home Office. Safelet only accept referrals for people supported under the *1948 National Assistance*

Act or who would be eligible under this Act if they lose entitlement to housing benefit.

Hosting schemes

A further recent innovation has been the development of *hosting*, or *placement* schemes. This arrangement involves identifying local households which might be able to offer a supportive environment to asylum seekers. Payments are made to these families, under the *1948 National Assistance Act*, to reflect accommodation and food expenses. Praxis, a voluntary organisation based in East London, has been actively involved in developing this model. Together with other community groups, it will also be involved in monitoring the effectiveness of these arrangements.

Among local authorities, there appears to be growing support for this model, recognising the advantages of cultural support and sustainability of such placements.

Conclusions

Good and poor practice in RSL provision for refugees and asylum seekers operate in close proximity. Most organisations provide more than basic housing management services. This reflects the fact that many asylum seekers need a much greater level of support than just access to housing for resettlement. This support is provided either as extended housing services or through partnerships with other agencies.

However, there are areas where, with little additional resource, significant improvements could be made to the breadth of service delivery. An example of a currently missed opportunity is the linkage of healthcare, particularly TB screening facilities, with existing housing projects. This would be a positive interpretation of the current emphasis on Best Value. There is substantial potential for enhancing policies and practices for the needs of female-headed refugee and asylum seeker households. While the majority of asylum seekers are male, the multiple problems experienced by many females and female-headed households require additional consideration and understanding by policy makers and service deliverers.

There are also pressures on RSLs to maximise the use of their existing stock in order to achieve an optimum balance between rental income and meeting housing need. Refugees and asylum seekers should feature within this process. The government White Paper, *Fairer, faster and firmer*, may appear to offer an opportunity to RSLs by directing asylum seekers to areas where there is hard-to-let stock. While this may appear attractive as a short-term resolution, the longer-term consequences may be less positive. That is not to say that RSLs should not be innovative and flexible with hard-to-let stock. However, any schemes should be developed on the basis of good practice rather than opportunism. A further area that might be further explored is an expanded use of the short-term leasing schemes currently operated by RSLs in conjunction with local authorities.

Of equal concern is that in some cases, the basics of housing management are not being performed to an acceptable level. Some projects fail to do so either because the resources needed to deliver the services are unsustainable, or because they operate on too narrow a focus which does not fully take into account the needs of users. Hostel accommodation provides a good example of shortfalls in service provision. Their use, as part of a coherent strategy for resettling asylum seekers, is widely advocated. Hostels offer the advantages of sustainability, while providing a focus around which support services can be delivered. However, successful provision is dependent on a much greater degree of cooperation and understanding among all parties than is currently the case.

The larger, generic organisations are better equipped to provide efficient management and good service delivery. But, as many of the examples show, it is the smaller community-based RSLs and RCO partners which provide the best practice in the crucial area of support services for asylum seekers and refugees. This is not to deny the value of the larger RSLs for clients who have low support needs and require few additional services to enable them to reconstruct their lives in a new environment. However, this may not satisfy the majority, and as Chapter 4 demonstrated, it is

important to recognise that refugees and asylum seekers are not an homogeneous group. For many, asylum and resettlement are complex and fundamental experiences. The demographic and social structure of households is extremely varied. Many will face long periods in temporary housing, may have language and/or skills problems and most will carry with them the trauma of flight and exile. These factors demand a particular style of housing management and provision, sensitive to their needs and which provides the foundation to build a new life.

7

Addressing future need

Future prospects

Significant levels of housing need exist among refugees and asylum seekers – a need emphasised both by individual households and the organisations working with them. Housing is not the sole requirement. The vast majority of these households enter the UK with few personal possessions, and have other social and cultural needs. However, housing attains special significance because it underpins other social, political and economic requirements, and influences health, education and employment. Refugees and asylum seekers stand a much greater chance of avoiding welfare dependency in a stable and adequate living environment, regardless of their length of stay within the UK. Policies and practices which create satisfactory housing provision are likely not only to benefit refugees and asylum seekers, but provide also a more cost-effective and sustainable service.

Building on the recommendations and good practice identified in earlier chapters, this chapter examines some of the preconditions to providing such a service for asylum seekers and refugees. Most of the recommendations relate to the structural factors of government policy, legislation and public resources which underpin service delivery. It is easy to be critical of the shortcomings in services delivered by RSLs and RCOs. At the same time, it is important to set these shortfalls in good practice in a wider structural framework. But there are also more specific recommendations for RSLs and RCOs working directly in the field which would, even within structural constraints, immeasurably improve the housing services to this client group.

A sustainable way forward is based on five key provisos:

- **Improving current practice in RSLs and RCOs working with refugees and asylum seekers**, especially with regard to awareness, collaboration and training programmes.
- **Removing some of the barriers in the perceptions of The Housing Corporation and RSLs working with this client group**.
- **Adopting a strategic approach to the resettlement process which operates through a system of local and national strategic action plans.**
- **Providing a coherent reception policy with staged accommodation** to take account of different levels of support needed in the process of resettlement.
- **Developing a coherent funding strategy for this sector which recognises both the short-term and long-term needs** of the client group and the range of agencies who should be resourced to deliver services such as housing.

Within this context, and in the light of the findings of the study, the last section of this chapter considers some of the implications of the government's policy White Paper, *Fairer, faster and firmer*.

Improving current practice

RSLs are uniquely placed to provide services to refugees and asylum seekers in ways that benefit all parties. RSLs can offer more efficient and effective housing services for this client group than local authorities from whom they have inherited this role. They work across local authority boundaries and often possess the relevant expertise to make informed strategic and operational plans. They also have the capacity to focus on the needs of specific groups such as refugees and asylum seekers, without the diversion of having to meet statutory obligations under the homelessness and other social legislation.

RSLs have a much better image and reputation among asylum seekers and their advocates than local authorities. This is largely because they are not directly associated with the statutory function of homelessness and are therefore viewed as independent. RSLs are also more likely to have their roots in the communities they serve (see Chapters 5 and 6), they command greater confidence and support and have relevant skills and expertise. The sector has developed a unique balance between performance and extended housing management and services. These are all benefits on which good practice can be enhanced.

But many issues within the current system need to be addressed if service provision by RSLs for refugees and asylum seekers is to be sustained and further improved. Although RSLs and RCOs currently offer much needed services, often under difficult conditions, the potential exists to achieve greater effectiveness, even within the current constraints.

Given that the role of RSLs is set to expand, this adds to the imperative for improvements in practice which this report has indicated. These obligations exist, irrespective of the outcome of the government review.

There are a number of areas where good practice should be improved and developed further. The Housing Corporation, along with other housing and support agencies, has a central role in establishing, disseminating and monitoring good practice.

Awareness

RSLs must enhance their understanding of the experiences and needs of refugees and asylum seekers. Currently the larger RSLs show little awareness of the ways in which they can

provide positive assistance for these households and their communities. The vast majority limit their input to the provision of permanent accommodation which is in short supply and outside the eligibility of many asylum seekers. Far more assistance could be provided through advice, support and collaboration. Many RSLs already deliver similar services under the Housing Plus banner. Significant additional benefits can be derived from extending these practices to refugees and asylum seekers, particularly in collaboration with RCOs.

RSL and RCO interface

The area of greatest potential to improve service delivery to refugees and asylum seekers lies in improved collaboration and partnership between RSLs and RCOs. This report highlights many instances of collaboration but these are often pragmatic and reactive, rather than planned and responsive. In some cases, the relationship is exploitative and some RCOs believe they are used to unlock resources but with little support for the communities themselves. There is a gulf in understanding between the two groups about their roles, the constraints within which they operate and what each can offer within a collaborative framework.

RSLs have the resources and expertise to provide efficiently managed housing while RCOs are best placed to provide the support services which are a vital element of social housing and the resettlement process. What is needed are well conceived partnerships which produce effective strategies and pooled resources to deliver comprehensive housing services to the asylum seeker and refugee communities which they serve.

Local authority/RSL partnership

Joint commissioning may produce the undesirable side-effect of marginalising the small RCOs which serve asylum seeker and refugee communities. To ensure this does not occur, improved structures for coordinating and monitoring the work of organisations dealing with refugees and asylum seekers need to be put in place. Local authorities and RSLs have begun to limit the number of organisations they accept as partners, an approach promoted by The Housing Corporation under the banner of joint commissioning. This means that a single, or perhaps two minority ethnic organisations may be chosen as the main vehicle(s) through which an authority/RSL might work. While this may rationalise resources, and encourage other BME associations and community groups to forge an alliance with the RSL working with the local authority, it may also marginalise smaller RCOs and the communities they serve. This trend may disproportionately affect RCOs which are invariably very small, lack the institutional capacity of better and longer established community groups, and are highly specific to the ethnic communities they serve. They do not have the leverage on local authorities and RSLs to ensure that their resources and the needs of their communities are fully taken into account. Their marginalisation may remain undetected by local authorities unless they have very close links across minority ethnic communities in their areas.

The need for networking

RCOs must fundamentally review and improve their networking capacity. Liaison between organisations representing minority ethnic communities is surprisingly poorly developed, despite the existence of agencies like the Federation of Black Housing Organisations (FBHO). This vacuum relates especially to RCOs, with problems such as duplication: "sometimes you find seven or eight RCOs working for one refugee community; playing the same role and applying for help from the same RSL and nobody gets anything" (Representative of Tamil Community Housing Association). The lack of adequate coordination between the RCOs dilutes their potential to make the best use of their expertise and to exert the maximum influence in the allocation of resources and the promotion of their policy objectives. A standing conference of RCOs and related organisations in the voluntary sector might be one way of improving networking and establishing effective links with related agencies. This might be linked to the established consultative machinery such as the Association of London Government (ALG) and Local Government Association.

The need for training

Better and more appropriate training is necessary for RSLs and RCOs in dealing with housing issues for asylum seekers and refugees. More housing-specific training may enable RCOs to make more informed decisions about whether or not to manage RSL-owned housing stock, and the skills and expertise needed to do so. Many RCOs do this out of necessity; training is required in vital areas of asset management, housing legislation, allocation and repair of social housing. Some RCOs are well intentioned but may not be offering their tenants a good service. This ultimately reflects badly on the RSL-owners who also have an interest in ensuring that partnerships with RCOs deliver effective and efficient services.

There is also a need for training for RSLs on ways of working with potential partners and the resources they can bring to improve housing services and support for asylum seekers and refugees. Some RSLs enter into arrangements to accommodate this group without fully appreciating the implications and the commitments for themselves, their partners or the service users. The services are not as responsive as they might be to clients' needs, and relationships between partners becomes fraught. This training should encompass such factors as: legislation concerning this client group; awareness of special social, cultural and psychological needs; and working with community organisations which often have fragile structures and capacities.

Removing barriers in perception by The Housing Corporation and RSLs

Resolving the dilemma between humanitarian purpose and efficiency is largely in the hands of central government and the statutory agencies. It is also an issue for The Housing Corporation and the RSLs because there are barriers in policy implementation which limit improvements to current ways of working.

The Housing Corporation

An important example is the Corporation's policy supporting black and minority ethnic housing associations, since refugee-based RSLs and RCOs are part of this constituency. More investment is needed in support, advice, training and financial resources to overcome some of the inertia in BME housing associations. Thus, in a survey of 52 London RCOs conducted in 1994 (HACT, 1994b), only three were RSLs in receipt of any Housing Corporation funding. Our own study reinforces the sense of marginalisation which RCOs have experienced by major institutions like The Housing Corporation, and the difficulties they face in expanding from a small base into credible housing agencies. The Corporation has regulatory requirements for registering new RSLs designed to ensure sound management control and a viable asset base. The need for assurance is not in question. On the other hand, there must be greater recognition that RCOs require a significant amount of nurturing and continued support if they are to develop into organisations fully able to deliver the current service standards expected of RSLs.

RSLs

It is also easy to criticise RSLs for adopting a relatively laissez-faire attitude to the provision of services to refugees and asylum seekers. However, they are products of the environment in which they operate and have been forced to modify their operations to ensure financial viability and to safeguard the interests of their existing tenants. The perceived risks of working with asylum seekers, as the study shows, are considerable, but it is a matter of perception.

If an asylum seeker household loses benefit entitlement or financial support under the *1948 National Assistance Act*, the worst that can happen is that an RSL might forego a limited amount of rental income while repossessing the property. Proactive RSLs offering resettlement support stand to lose more – staff time and expertise which could be rendered worthless overnight. For example, one RSL reported how it had provided considerable resettlement support over a period of time only to find a whole street of families traumatically deported suddenly and without warning.

There are risks, though they are not substantial, and from one perspective, there are few obvious incentives for RSLs to invest resources in asylum seekers. For both the Corporation and the RSLs, the huge backlog of appeal and pending applications and the uncertainty of government policy further intensify the perception that committing resources to this group may not make sound financial and managerial sense. Within such an environment it is difficult to expect organisations proactively to develop a coherent body of good practice.

Nevertheless, despite the constraints, some RSLs have been remarkably innovative in the accommodation and support they have provided to refugees and asylum seekers. Their perception has been a positive one. Rooted in the communities they serve and working in partnership with other service providers, they recognise that provision for asylum seekers and refugees fits within their mandate and purpose. As previous chapters have illustrated, these RSLs offer many examples of good practice and positive perceptions in adverse circumstances. With a change of perception, little risk and modest investment, other RSLs, currently delivering well below their potential capacity for innovative and sustainable projects, could reverse this position.

A strategic approach to resettlement

This underutilisation of RSL potential needs to be considered within the context of the policy vacuum and the absence of a strategic framework for planning resettlement. Both a local and a national framework of strategic action plans is needed.

Local strategic framework

Local authorities have an important role to play in coordinating the provision of services and accommodation for asylum seekers and refugees. The effectiveness of this role, particularly in London, has been raised in this study, and service delivery is fragmented. Local authorities are sometimes obstructive rather than constructive and this can seriously diminish the chances of refugees and asylum seekers to receive a satisfactory service.

This problem is evident, to varying degrees, across all of our case study areas. Even authorities like Manchester and Birmingham where, despite a commitment to a coordinating role with service providers and a corporate approach within the authority, the practical outcomes have been pragmatic and unsystematic. These characteristics are particularly marked in London where, in the absence of a strategic body, there is little coordinated operational planning across the capital. Some London authorities have worked in concert, forming consortia to house asylum seekers; but this has been the exception rather than the norm. At officer level liaison between authorities may work well but this is inconsistent. There is resentment where local authorities have 'dumped' their asylum seekers in neighbouring boroughs or even further afield. There is confusion and inconsistency in the policies and practices adopted by local authorities.

This situation works against the effective reception and accommodation of refugees and asylum seekers and leads to inefficient use of already scarce resources. Front-line service providers – the RSLs and RCOs – lack a framework within which to plan and coordinate service provision. The knowledge and expertise which exists at officer level in local authorities, often developed in dealing with the crisis of the last two years, is not effectively used.

A clear need exists for coherent local level action strategies, or at least a coordinating framework, in areas most affected by asylum seeker demand for housing. Local authorities are best placed to organise these initiatives, involving the statutory and voluntary sectors and RSLs.

The action plans should reflect local authority housing strategies, but establish the needs of refugees and asylum seekers within a locality and identify the resources available to them. The plans would draw upon the knowledge and expertise of local communities, the voluntary sector and link with key local resources, for example, colleges, health facilities, religious groups and cultural centres. These plans would need to make some assessment of demand and the distribution of refugee and asylum seekers to ensure the most appropriate service availability. Local action plans would go some way to overcome the current lack of understanding of the needs and difficulties experienced by refugee and asylum seeker households.

The corporate policy frameworks adopted by Birmingham and Manchester provide models for such an approach, but they lack an action planning impetus. It is crucial that mechanisms are created to sustain the action plans and frameworks. The experience of Oxford's Multi-Agency Forum, which meets on a quarterly basis, well-supported by the statutory and voluntary partners, provides an example of how this can be achieved.

National strategic framework

A national strategic framework is also required for the capacity of RSLs and RCOs to be realised.

A viable way forward is for central government to take on the responsibility for funding a coherent national policy through a responsible coordinating body. Such a body should include: The Housing Corporation as a major partner; representation from the local authority sector; other expert agencies such as the Refugee Council; possibly other representatives of the RCO/voluntary sector drawn from the proposal for a Standing Conference of RCOs (see p 50, 'The need for networking').

While the government promises a coherent approach to policy and a new body to implement policy in the 1998 White Paper, it is not yet clear how this will be achieved. The penultimate section of this chapter (p 54) discusses some of the potential and the limitations of what has been outlined. The proposals fall short of a comprehensive framework for developing and coordinating national policy. A body geared solely towards restriction and control, rather than drawing on the strengths and capabilities of all the service providers, will not produce an efficient use of resources nor an equitable service for asylum seekers.

A coherent approach to reception and staged housing

Unlike some European partners, Britain currently lacks a coherent reception policy for asylum seekers. Neither specially provided hostels with a range of support services needed by new arrivals, nor staged 'move-on' accommodation are provided. A structured approach to initial reception is central to an effective immigration policy, and would be cost-effective in the medium and long term. More importantly, sensitively delivered reception accommodation and support plays a key role in re-establishing the independence and self-sufficiency of asylum seekers.

The White Paper, *Fairer, faster and firmer*, makes proposals for a coordinated reception process, centralised within a new government agency whose aim will be to provide accommodation and basic services. This proposal has many extremely unsatisfactory elements, which are discussed on p 54.

Reception centres

Irrespective of the length of time asylum seekers await an application decision, it is more sustainable and cost-effective to provide reception facilities which enable them to lead a secure and dignified existence. If this is not achieved in a planned and coordinated manner, service delivery is fragmented and the subsequent costs are often greater.

The term 'reception' is often perceived in a pejorative sense, linked to an ineffective system of central control and a perversely imposed dependency. This has discouraged the development of good practice. There is a critical role for reception in providing adequate facilities which offer support and nurturing for those who require it, and advice and advocacy for those who may be more independent. Reception should be, as the name suggests, a short-term, flexible facility which provides a bridge to independence. Reception facilities should be developed and managed with the full cooperation and support of local community groups and representative agencies who are best placed to offer additional support, advice and advocacy.

The current approach adopted by RSLs like Refugee Housing Association, of initial reception, supplemented by second- and possibly third-stage accommodation, offers a sound model for achieving the objectives of well-delivered reception facilities.

Move-on accommodation

Provision for adequate move-on accommodation into independent living is also required. This is essential if the initial staged services are not to become clogged, thus rendering them ineffective. Once again, RSLs are well-placed to provide and manage this stage of housing provision through the development and management of Rent Guarantee/ Deposit Schemes (RAGDS). Such accommodation might make use of the private rented sector where there are suitable dwellings available, of course.

Provision must be sensitive to the fact that a significant number of asylum seekers may require nothing more than appropriate accommodation, without any accompanying support. To ignore this not only places the users into unsuitable environments, but also constitutes a waste of valuable resources.

The effectiveness of move-on accommodation would be greatly enhanced if the process for determining asylum claims was accelerated. Removing protracted uncertainty would help to reduce the problems of congestion within existing housing stock.

The needs of elderly refugees, although comparatively small at present, are likely to increase as greater numbers of refugees and asylum seekers are settling in the UK. These needs are currently neglected at present.

Funding

Funding is at the core of developing a sustainable system of housing provision for refugees and asylum seekers.

Short- versus long-term needs

At present, the dependence on short-term, person-specific funding, such as that generated by the *1948 National Assistance Act*, inhibits effective forward planning. As the study shows, this produces tensions between local authorities, who are only willing to commit funding to projects for a year until the government review is finalised, and RSLs who generally seek much longer-term arrangements. This level of uncertainty applies to other sources of revenue funding which tend to be short-term (often annual), such as Supported Housing Management Grant (SHMG) and grants from organisations such as the London Boroughs Grants Unit (LBGU).

This situation prevents long-term business planning which would encourage RSLs to invest in the rehabilitation of existing buildings or the construction of new accommodation for asylum seekers and refugees. These constraints apply most severely to hostel and reception centre provision, where quality standards may suffer and overall supply is insufficient because longer-term funding arrangements are not in place.

More beneficial would be a special fund distributed via The Housing Corporation which would, subject to satisfactory performance, guarantee revenue funding for a number of years. This could be achieved by reallocating to the Corporation the 'housing component' of the funds currently being spent by the Home Office to reimburse SSDs. Not only would this enable services to be placed on a more stable footing, it would also increase the potential for accessing private finance, perhaps through the Private Finance Initiative. This would allow greater independence and financial security for hostel providers, without increasing the government's spending targets.

To a limited extent, the government's proposals will lead to a more coordinated funding regime. Since this will be controlled by central government, the suspicion must be that this will merely be an expenditure control process rather than a coherent funding strategy for this sector of social housing need.

Access to funds

Another problematic aspect of the current funding regime is that access is heavily geared in favour of larger, more established organisations. This can be divisive and discriminatory because the smaller RCOs aspiring to expand find it the hardest to successfully plug into resource networks. They are insufficiently established to bid for Corporation

funds, for example, or other public sources. Yet, in many cases, they play a crucial role in supporting asylum seekers and refugee communities. They need to engage with a system which is supportive and facilitating rather than one which is adversarial and competitive.

Fairer, faster and firmer

The publication of the White Paper, *Fairer, faster and firmer*, in July 1988, outlined the parameters for future refugee and asylum seeker policy. Irrespective of changes in national policy framework, some of the proposals and initiatives outlined above can be developed. On the other hand, because policy is under fundamental review, these proposals are also a contribution to key areas of the review currently being conducted.

The proposals conceived by the government and now to be enacted in the 1999 Bill, will have profound implications for asylum seekers and refugees, and for the service providers examined in this study. Many of the government's proposals will, we believe, have a negative effect on both those seeking asylum and those providing for them. The final section of this chapter, therefore, reviews some of the government's main recommendations in the White Paper and the 1999 Bill in the light of the findings and proposals of our own study. In this way, we provide a critique of many of the government's recommendations while suggesting how many of its objectives could be taken forward in a more humane, sensitive and cost-effective way.

The groups contacted for this research indicated widespread anticipation of radical reform of asylum policies. This would have involved measures geared towards greater effectiveness in processing applications, delivering greater sensitivity in the decisions taken, and restoring more humane responses to those remaining in the UK.

However, the White Paper proposals largely accord with existing policy by retaining tight entry controls and emphasising the achievement of efficiency. Having implemented the previous government's policies since coming to power in May 1997, the regime is set to remain geared towards reducing the numbers of asylum seekers coming to the UK, and exercising much greater control over those who are admitted.

This White Paper follows in the wake of the government's Comprehensive Spending Review and the intention of continued commitment to earlier Conservative public spending limits. Indeed one of the stated objectives of the White Paper is to contain the costs of the asylum system.

The proposed measures will make the experience of asylum seeking as daunting as possible, in order to reinforce the principle of deterrence. A central plank of this strategy has been to reinforce the principal of excluding many categories of asylum seekers from welfare entitlements, enacted in 1996. This relates directly to the provision of benefits and the allocation of social housing – the subject of this research. In this context, this study is both timely and crucial, since a major proposal of the White Paper is the extension of hostel accommodation, which may directly impact on the activities of RSLs, as follows:

- Support will be provided separately from the existing statutory benefits arrangements, and will be available only where it is clearly necessary while an application is awaiting decision or appeal.
- The administration of a new accommodation and support scheme for asylum seekers will require new national machinery to plan and coordinate provision, obtaining information from around the country and purchasing residential places either directly or by contracting with local agencies. The budget and the machinery for administering it will be operated by the Home Office.
- Support for asylum seekers will no longer be funded by cash payments. The government intends to explore the extent to which support might be provided through vouchers or other non-cash means, so as to control further the costs of the asylum system.
- Accommodation will be provided on a no-choice basis, with no cash payment for this purpose being made to the asylum seeker. Asylum seekers would be expected to take what is offered. They will not be able to pick and choose where they are accommodated, which

normally takes into account the value of linking to existing communities and the support of voluntary and community groups.

- Basic needs will also be met where there is a genuine risk of hardship, including food and other living essentials, as well as facilities to enable asylum seekers properly to pursue their applications.
- The 1948 Act will be amended to make clear that SSDs should not carry the burden of looking after asylum seekers. This role will fall to the new national support machinery.
- The body responsible for obtaining and allocating accommodation would also be responsible for assessing whether applicants were in genuine need either by doing so itself or by contracting out the process to another agency.
- The government envisages contracting with a range of providers to secure accommodation, including voluntary bodies, housing associations, local authorities and the private sector. The government is particularly concerned to explore ways of harnessing the energy and expertise of voluntary and independent sector bodies in providing the safety net.
- Local authorities' current responsibilities to asylum seekers under the homelessness legislation will be removed and replaced by these new arrangements, but they will be expected to assist wherever possible (for example, by making available any spare accommodation on a contractual basis).

These proposals will impact significantly on the activity of RSLs. In such a regime, the role of RSLs could be much expanded from their current level of involvement. The opportunity to enter contractual arrangements will be attractive to a number of RSLs, particularly those which, to date, have not offered services to refugees and asylum seekers. The potential to use vacant, available dwellings, with guaranteed income, may well provide the incentive to using the most hard-to-let and poorest quality housing. There must be concern that, under these proposals, standards may fall further, unless there is rigorously applied quality control. Equally, the proposals envisage substantial hostel provision. As the previous chapter shows, this is already a problematic form of provision accommodating the most vulnerable of asylum seekers.

The Refugee Council speculates, "the proposed 'safety net' support system is likely to hit asylum seekers badly and risks building up a massive problem of social exclusion. It appears that the Government has chosen the ... most ... complicated system of support" (Refugee Council, July 1998). If this proves to be true, the prospect of large-scale RSL participation may prove less attractive when the details of the cashless safety net and management structures are announced. The proposals potentially cut across many of the principles which RSLs stand for in the services they offer.

Of equal concern are the proposed controls over the asylum seekers' choice of where they might be housed. This control mechanism will be counter-productive if individuals and households are accommodated away from their community and the support network of family and friends. As our research shows, alongside most research on this population, proximity to co-ethnic or co-national communities is often a vital element in the settlement process.

In addition, the White Paper implies that an objective is to relieve housing pressure on areas of very heavy demand and housing shortage. If refugee and asylum seeker households are only hard-to-let dwellings, this could undermine effective resettlement and actively contribute to the process of social exclusion. Again, the study reveals a tendency, not widespread as yet, for some RSLs to use asylum seekers as the opportunity to off-load hard-to-let and short-life properties. The danger of the new proposals is an increase in the perception of asylum seekers and refugees as people with little choice who will have to accept housing whatever its quality.

Since the completion of this report, the government have published the *1999 Immigration and Asylum Bill*. This has, in effect, taken forward many of the measures contained in the White Paper, *Fairer, faster and firmer* which we discuss in Chapter 7 of the report. At the point of publication, the Bill has received its second reading and is about to enter its committee stage. Although one should not rule out the possibility of further changes being introduced, any alterations are likely to be at the margins; the government's intentions seem clear. The main thrust of the Bill, as was the White Paper, is the introduction of measures to exclude and deter refugees and asylum seekers.

As expected, the Bill introduces a new Immigration Services Commissioner whose responsibility will be to "promote good practice by those who provide immigration advice or immigration services" (Section 62 (3)). The responsibility placed on local authorities by the *1948 National Assistance Act* is repealed, with the onus transferring to the Secretary of State, who *may* provide, or arrange provision of, support for asylum seekers or their dependants. However, this is only where they appear to be destitute or in danger of becoming destitute. In practice, this would include the vast majority of asylum seekers who enter the UK with little or no material wealth. The Bill also specifies that the accommodation to be provided will be of a temporary nature and further emphasises that any locational preference expressed by asylum seekers will not be material to the rehousing decision. Indeed, the Secretary of State must have regard to "the desirability, in general, of providing accommodation in areas in which there is a ready supply of accommodation" (Section 76 1(b)).

As feared, the indication is that asylum seekers will be located in areas where housing is less in demand and more readily available. Section 82 of the Bill enables the designation of local authority areas as *reception zones*, which are likely to be in areas of overprovision of social housing, for example the North East. Our concern is that these are likely to be in areas of high existing social deprivation which may not necessarily have the infrastructure or community support to sustain an influx. Existing research indicates that where, in the past, refugees have been subjected to a policy of deliberate dispersal, they inevitably relocate in areas which offer greater support. However, within the Bill, there are provisions to exclude asylum seekers from support if they leave the accommodation with which they were provided.

In general terms, the Bill offers little comfort to asylum seekers or those involved in working with them. The concerns raised following the issue of *Fairer, faster and firmer* remain as outlined in our report. The danger is that in the proposed reform of the process of dealing with asylum seekers, the government will serve only to extend social exclusion, increase the effects of residualisation and potentially fuel the effects of racism.

In short, the new proposals are not likely to produce an early resolution to the uncertainty which has blighted policy and practice in this area. Whatever the final detail, there appears little prospect of significant additional resources to meet the needs of refugees and asylum seekers. The onus will continue to be on services using existing innovation, sensitivity and expertise. Such a combination points inexorably towards the model of partnership and collaboration between RSLs and RCOs such as those examined in this study. While practice falls short of expectations at times, we have few doubts in the potential of this approach to deliver the desired objectives. It is therefore reasonable to assume that these organisations will continue to operate in the vanguard of refugee services.

Conclusion

The atmosphere of anti-immigrant rhetoric and negative publicity has a debilitating effect on service delivery, despite the innovation and commitment of many agencies and individuals. An ironic illustration is that some agencies who have developed good initiatives or display good practice are either nervous or eager *not* to publicise their work, concerned that publicity could backfire politically or have a negative impact on fundraising. Alternatively, there was concern that it could generate additional demand for services which they would be unable to meet.

This is not the sort of environment which nurtures competence and good practice – it generates misunderstanding and misinformation. This is a major barrier facing the organisations and their users covered by this study. Refugees and asylum seekers are a diverse group, perhaps sharing a common experience, but with widely differing needs and aspirations. Many refugees and asylum seekers need help and support to rebuild their lives and make their case to resettle without the fear of persecution. Most refugees bring with them highly developed skills and expertise from responsible positions held in their country of origin.

However, they are inaccurately portrayed as helpless. This may be motivated by good intent in the campaign for additional resources, but the negative impact is to mask the huge and often untapped potentialities of the group. This is but one example of where misunderstanding, or inaccurate assumptions, can lead to reduced quality and diminished performance. Service delivery strategies which do not provide refugees with opportunities to participate and become empowered are likely to be far less effective.

This chapter has presented some of the main structural elements which must underpin policy in this field. Clearer and more positive policies are key to developing a more positive image of refugees and asylum seekers.

These elements are:

- improving current practice
- removing barriers in perception by The Housing Corporation and RSLs
- strategic approach to resettlement
- coherent approach to reception and staged housing
- funding strategy.

Once these essential foundations are in place, RSLs and RCOs will be far better placed to work together to deliver the level of professional and humane services that are the hallmark of the social housing sector in the UK and to provide the quality of experience that refugees and asylum seekers have the right to expect.

Recommendations

Introduction

Policy uncertainty in central government has destabilised and severely constrained housing services for refugees and asylum seekers. Devising a system which offers an acceptable balance between support for asylum seekers and efficiency has proved difficult; there are pragmatic tensions between political expediency and humanitarian purpose. There can be no reliable indicators of future numbers, nationalities, family sizes or circumstances. Meaningful strategic planning is difficult.

Yet the UK will continue to receive substantial numbers of asylum seekers, and housing policy together with good practice in service delivery must respond to this demand.

To this end, this chapter draws together the findings of the study. The recommendations which follow are key aspects of policy strategy and practice which, taken together, will help to provide a coherent and equitable framework for the reception and resettlement of refugees and asylum seekers.

The recommendations are designed primarily for RSLs and The Housing Corporation since, although relatively few RSLs actively provide for this client group at present, they are increasingly significant providers – a role set to expand under the government's White Paper proposals in *Fairer, faster, firmer*. This report has identified considerable variability in the aims, role and practices of RSLs and the quality of provision made for refugees and asylum seekers. The recommendations aim to assist RSLs, as the major providers in the future, in developing and enhancing good practice. In this way a more effective and efficient service can be provided which is sensitive to the unique needs of this group.

Strategy and policy

- There is an urgent need for a coherent national policy framework for the reception and resettlement of refugees and asylum seekers. This needs to be implemented by central government in conjunction primarily with The Housing Corporation and the voluntary sector, and should also include local authorities (p 52, 'National strategic framework').

- A strategic approach to housing and other services is required which focuses on the role of RSLs and RCOs as the primary providers of housing and related services for refugees and asylum seekers. This should be operated through a system of local action plans in close liaison with local authorities (p 51, 'Local strategic framework' and p 26).

- In the context of housing and support services, the strategy should recognise changing housing needs at different phases of the reception and resettlement process. This would help to ensure a range of provision is conceived, enable providers to identify where they can best contribute to housing provision, and if properly managed, would remove some of the blockages in the present system (pp 52-3, 'A coherent approach').

- RSLs and The Housing Corporation need to develop greater awareness and knowledge of the issues relating to refugees and asylum seekers and the diversity of the population. RSLs should consider the need to develop policies for this client group. These objectives might be achieved through training (see below) and/or the production of appropriate literature, and through closer contact with RCOs (p 26, 'RSLs – refugee and asylum seeker needs'; p 39, 'Access'; p 49, 'Awareness'; pp 50-1, 'Removing barriers').

- The area of greatest improvements in service delivery to refugees and asylum seekers by RSLs lies in closer collaboration and improved partnership with RCOs and the communities they serve. A perception of RCOs as agents rather than partners needs to be overcome (p 27, 'RCOs – barriers and opportunities'; p 41, 'Partnerships'; p 49, 'RSL and RSO interface').

- Local authorities must consider the broader implications of their strategies for selecting joint commissioning partners. Limiting the numbers may have advantages in terms of the concentration of resources, but it may be exclusionary and divisive (p 26, 'RSLs – power structures'; pp 49-50, 'Local authority/RSL partnership').

- RCOs urgently need to improve their networking and communication skills. They are currently marginalised and misunderstood. This should include the establishment of a national forum for organisations providing services for refugees and asylum seekers, to facilitate the sharing of good practice and expertise and to develop strategic policies and plans (p 27; p 50, 'The need for networking').

- Better and more appropriate training must be undertaken by RCOs and RSLs dealing with housing issues for this client group.

  Additional training is needed for RSL staff directly involved in assessing and providing services for asylum seeker and refugee tenants, preferably involving service users in training sessions. Training should address, in particular, the development of an enhanced sensitivity in access and allocation policies (p 27, 'Training'; p 39, 'Access'; pp 40-1, 'Empowerment').

  For RCOs, training is needed to improve institutional capacity, financial and management skills. Housing-specific training will better enable them to decide whether to manage housing stock. It is also necessary to overcome the significant variations in RCO

performance standards in housing management (p 27, 'RCOs – barriers'; p 27, 'Training'; p 50, 'The need for training').

- RSLs and The Housing Corporation should explore the means to share and disseminate good practice in this area (pp 27-8; pp 48-50, 'Improving current practice'; p 57, 'Conclusion').

- RSLs and RCOs should recognise and mobilise the range of personal resources which are often present within refugee communities. These are frequently underutilised and could be better employed by improving the support and providing greater encouragement for involvement in service delivery (p 26, 'RSLs – refugee'; pp 40-1, 'Empowerment').

- RSLs need to be aware of the current and future housing requirements of elderly refugees. The need for additional support mechanisms must be recognised and resourced (p 19, 'Problems with accommodation'; p 53, 'Move-on accommodation').

- RSLs should give more consideration to developing specific refugee-related initiatives (eg tailoring Housing Plus projects to the specific needs of this group), in order to develop and enhance the skills, self-sufficiency and aspirations of the refugees and asylum seekers. Exploring some of the initiatives drawn from RSLs delivering good practice would be an excellent starting point (pp 40-1, 'Empowerment').

- RSLs should also consider how best to facilitate the expression of cultural and social needs of asylum seekers and refugees (pp 19-20, 'Social isolation'; p 20, 'Identified improvements'). Again, initiatives drawn from RSLs delivering good practice provides a valuable starting point (pp 34-5, 'Providence Row' and 'St Mungos'; pp 40-1, 'Empowerment').

- RSLs should explore ways in which they might engage with communities and residents in neighbourhoods where they accommodate significant numbers of refugee and asylum seeker tenant. These processes might help to reduce the tensions that are sometimes experienced in local communities (pp 34-5, 'Providence Row' and 'St Mungos').

- Despite funding constraints, RSLs can access financial resources to make improved provision for this client group. RSLs need to ensure that tightening of financial criteria does not exclude potentially valuable partnerships with RCOs (p 26, 'Financial constraints...'; p 27, 'RSLs providing...'; pp 53-4, 'Short- versus').

- New initiatives are needed to support RCOs in accessing funds for the provision of housing and related services (p 26, 'Small and/or...'; p 54, 'Access to funds').

- RSLs should examine how best to maximise the use of their existing stock and other procurement options, for example, short-term leasing (p 46, 'Safelet scheme').

- RSLs have considerable capacity and flexibility to use their finances to assist new and existing tenants thought to be 'risk categories', at little risk or cost to themselves. These opportunities should be more fully investigated (pp 39-40, 'Finance'; pp 53-4, 'Short- versus...').

Operational

- The most significant area for operational improvement is in housing access and allocation procedures (p 19).

- Improved complaints procedures systems are needed for refugees and asylum seekers tenants. The use of external bodies, such as independent visitors or RCOs, to offer advice and support should be encouraged (pp 40-1, 'Empowerment').

- RCOs and RSLs should be aware of the need to produce material in translation for those refugees and asylum seekers for whom English is not their first language (pp 18-20, 'Experience of...'; pp 40-1, 'Empowerment').

- RSLs, in particular, should develop sensitive access and allocations policies which reflect the special needs of refugees and asylum seekers.

- RSLs and RCOs should develop more responsive and easily accessible means of tenant participation (pp 19-20, 'Social isolation'; p 20, 'Participation'; pp 40-1, 'Empowerment').

References and further reading

[*Excluding* press cuttings, other ephemera and reports, briefing notes and documents etc of agencies and organisations interviewed as part of the field investigation.]

Afoun, P. (1997) Discussion Paper on 'Reception of refugees', Presented to a meeting of the Refugee Housing Association Advisory Panel, London, 25 July.

Agathangalou, A. (1989) *The housing situation of refugees*, A descriptive data report presented at Refugee Housing Forum, commissioned by the Refugee Council.

Ahmed, M., F., Adan, O.M, and Dualeh, M.A.A (1991) *Somali community of Tower Hamlets: A demographic survey*, London.

ALG (Association of London Government) (1996) *No place to call home: Report and recommendations for London local authorities on the implementation of the new legislation affecting refugees and asylum seekers*, London: ALG and Refugee Council.

ALG (1998) *Weekly statistics of asylum seekers presenting to London boroughs*, compiled by London Borough of Hammersmith and Fulham.

All Party Group on Homelessness and Housing Need (1997) *Briefing Paper – Who is responsible for housing asylum seekers?*, 10 December, London: CHAS.

AMA (Association of Metropolitan Authorities) (1991) *A strategy for housing refugees*, London: AMA.

Bariso, E.U. (1997) *The Horn of Africa health research project: An assessment of the accessibility and appropriateness of health care*, London: North Thames Regional Health Authority.

Battaglia, D. (1998) *Rent-in-Advance Guarantee Scheme – End of project report*, London: Refugee Council.

Bayley, R. (1997) 'No place like home', *Roof*, November/December, pp 34-6.

Bell, J. (1993) *Ugandan refugees: A study of housing conditions and the circumstances of children*, London: Community Development Foundation.

Biggs, M. (1997) *No way in: Housing rights of asylum seekers, refugees and people from abroad*, London: Housing Law Training Centre.

Bloch, A. (1996a) *Beating the barriers: The employment and training needs of refugees in Newham*, London: London Borough of Newham.

Bloch, A. (1996b) 'Refugees in Newham', in T. Butler and M. Rustin (eds) *Rising in the East: The regeneration of East London*, London: Lawrence & Wishart.

Borkum, S. (1997?) *The housing situation of Latin American refugees living in London*, London: CARILA, Latin American Welfare Group.

BRC (British Refugee Council) (1987) *Settling for a future: Proposals for a British policy on refugees*, London: BRC.

BRC (1988) *Working together: Refugees and local authorities in London*, London: BRC.

BRC (1989) *The housing situation of refugees*, London: BRC.

Buckley, C. (1996) *Safe havens*, London: London Federation of Housing Associations.

Buckley, C. (1997) *Safe haven: What housing associations can do to assist asylum seekers*, London: NFHA.

Carey-Wood, J., Duke, K., Karn, V. and Marshall, T. (1995) *The settlement of refugees in Britain*, Home Office Research Study 141, London: HMSO.

Carter, M. (1996) 'The squeeze on asylum seekers', *Poverty*, vol 94, Summer, pp 9-11.

Cervi, B. (1995) 'Gimme shelter', *Community Care*, no 1065, 28 April, pp 16-17.

Cohen, R. (1994) *Frontiers of identity: The British and the others*, London: Longman.

Compass Partnership (1997) *The Bosnia Project: Stage 2 Evaluation of the Interagency Bosnia Project*, London: Compass Partnership.

Duke, K. and Marshall, T. (1995) *Vietnamese refugees since 1982*, Home Office Research Study 142, London: HMSO.

El-Sohl, F. (1991) 'Somalis in London's East End: a community striving for recognition', *New Community*, vol 17, no 4, pp 539-52.

Field, S. (1985) *Resettling refugees: The lessons of research*, Home Office Research Study 87, London: HMSO.

Finlay, R. and Reynolds, J. (1987) *Social work and refugees: A handbook on working with people in exile in the UK*, London: National Extension College and Refugee Action.

Francis, J. (1996) 'Easy target', *Community Care*, 5-10 January, pp 14-15.

Gallagher, J. (1997) *The Housing Act 1996 and the Asylum and Immigration Act 1996: Shelter and the CRE Guidance on Eligible and Qualifying Persons*, London: Shelter and CRE.

Gammell, H.M., Ndahiro, A., Nicholon, N. and Windsor, J. (1992) *Refugees (political asylum seekers): Service provision and access to the NHS*, London: Newham HealthCare.

HACT (Housing Associations Charitable Trust) (1994a) *Housing needs of refugees in the North*, London: HACT.

HACT (1994b) *Housing issues facing refugee communities in London: A survey*, London: HACT [authors: Ayom Wol, Liz Firth and Reena Mukherji].

Home Office (1998) *Fairer, faster and firmer: A modern approach to immigration and asylum*, Government White Paper Cmd 4018, London: The Stationery Office.

Housing Corporation Circular (January 1997) *R3 – 04/97*, 'Letting to certain persons [from] abroad', London: The Housing Corporation.

Housing Corporation Circular (January 1998) *R3 – 34/97*, 'Temporary lettings to asylum seekers', London: The Housing Corporation.

Humm, J. (1996) *Settling in Cambridge: The refugee experience*, London: Refugee Action.

Iraqi Community Association (1996) *Now we are here: A survey of the profile, structure, needs, hopes, and aspiration of the Iraqi community in Britain*, London: Iraqi Community Association.

Joly, D. (1996) *Haven or hell: Asylum policy in Europe*, London: Macmillan.

Latin American Welfare Group (1997) *The housing situation of Latin American refugees living in London*, London: HACT and Latin American Welfare Group.

London Federation of Housing Associations (1996) *Safe havens: What housing associations can do to assist asylum seekers*, London: Federation of Housing Associations [author: Colin Buckley].

Lumley, R. (1993) 'The effects of the asylum and immigration appeals legislation on housing rights', *Housing Review*, vol 42, no 3, pp 39-40.

Majke, L. (1991) 'Assessing refugee assistance organisations in the United States and the United Kingdom', *Journal of Refugee Studies*, vol 4, no 3, pp 267-83.

Marsh, A. and Sangster, A. (1998) *Paving the way: Supporting black and minority ethnic housing associations*, Bristol: The Policy Press.

Means, R. and Sangster, A. (1998) *In search of a home: An evaluation of refugee housing advice and development workers*, Bristol: The Policy Press.

Medical Foundation (1997) *Past misery, present muddle: Council by council survey of assistance to asylum seekers one year on*, London: Medical Foundation.

Mukherji, R. (1994) 'Housing issues facing refugees in London: a survey', *Housing Review*, vol 43, no 3, pp 103-4.

Quiglan, D. (1993) *Housing provision for refugees*, York: University of York, Centre for Housing Policy.

RC (Refugee Council) (1995) *Homelessness and asylum: The Asylum and Immigration Appeals Act 1993: A guide for housing authorities*, London: RC.

RC (1996) *Refugee resources in the UK*, London: RC.

RC (1997a) *The development of a refugee settlement policy in the UK – Refugee Council Working Paper*, London: RC.

RC (1997b) *Accommodation for asylum seekers: A proposal*, London: RC.

RC (1997c) *An agenda for action: Challenges for refugee settlement in the UK*, London: RC.

RC (1998) *Briefing on the government's Immigration and Asylum White Paper*, July, London: RC.

Refugee Housing Association (1997) *Developing a national strategy for the reception of refugees*, London: Refugee Housing Association [author: Melan Fardouee].

Robinson, V. (1985) 'The Vietnamese reception and resettlement programme in the UK: Rhetoric and reality', *Ethnic Groups*, vol 6, pp 305-30.

Robinson, V. (1993a) 'British policy towards the settlement of ethnic groups: an empirical evaluation of the Vietnamese programme, 1979-88', in V. Robinson (ed) *The international refugee crisis: British and Canadian responses*, London: Macmillan.

Robinson, V. (1993b) 'Marching into the middle classes? The long term resettlement of East African Asians in the UK', *Journal of Refugee Studies*, vol 6, no 3, pp 230-47.

Robinson, V. (1999) 'Weaknesses in the provision of services for refugees in the UK: the case study of Wales', *Journal of Refugee Studies*, vol 12, no 2, forthcoming.

Somali Islington Community and Islington Health 2000 (1996) *Islington Somali Community survey*, Islington.

UNHCR (1997) *The state of the world's refugees*, Geneva: UNHCR.

UNHCR.www (1998) *Refworld website – UK country report*, Geneva: UNHCR.

Watson, M. and Hooper, N. (1997) *Home Office Statistical Bulletin: Asylum statistics 1996*, London: Research and Statistics Directorate.

West, C. and Lemos, G. (1996) *Flair in the community*, London: NFHA.

Zetter, R. (1999) 'International perspectives on refugee assistance', Chapter 3 in A. Ager (ed) *Refugees: Contemporary perspectives on the experience of refugees*, London: Cassell.

A

Appendix A: Scope, context and the research setting

Introduction

Because of the difficulties of conducting research on refugees and asylum seekers, relatively little is known about them and their housing needs. This is in marked contrast with research of the ethnic minority population in the UK as a whole. While the experience of migration provides a unifying characteristic, and in the case of asylum seekers and refugees this is more specifically *forced migration*, in practice there are divergent experiences between different ethnic groups, how they have arrived and how they have settled.

For service providers, such as RSLs, the lack of knowledge of reception and resettlement needs and experiences are barriers to identifying good practice. The is highlighted by the rapid changes in the statutory, judicial and policy framework in recent years.

Within this context, the scope of this study is defined by two factors. For The Housing Corporation and RSL providers, current national policies and statutory provision, particularly the curtailing of entry and welfare rights of refugees and asylum seekers since 1993 and the impact on eligibility for housing, define an immediate, practice-based context. But this study is also located within a more general context of other recent research about refugees and asylum seekers in Britain and the role which service providers play in the processes of resettlement, socioeconomic integration and specialist needs for this minority and often marginalised social group.

National policies, statutory framework and impacts on RSLs
Policy context

Britain has a long history of hosting refugees and affording asylum, well before the international conventions and human rights declarations of the last half century. Britain is one of the original 13 states party to the Geneva Convention of 1951 and the Protocol in 1967 which define the basic framework of norms which signatories agree to adopt when dealing with asylum seekers and refugees. Although Britain's humanitarian stance has always been circumscribed by self-interest and wider considerations about immigration, in common with most other developed countries, it has adopted a relatively benign attitude – until recently. By and large, it has honoured the cardinal principle of non-refoulement, and it has, with conditions, accepted most of the Articles of the Convention as regards the basic entitlements of refugees. Between 1985 and 1996, 67,000 heads of households were permitted to stay, of which 12,000 were granted full refugee status.

Britain had accepted both programme or quota refugees – for example, Hungarians, Ugandan Asians, Vietnamese, whose entry and settlement could in theory be carefully regulated – and also spontaneously arriving refugees.

But towards the end of the 1980s, this situation changed fundamentally and highly discriminatory legislation and policies were introduced. The stimulus was domestic political objectives and aspirations, combined with fears about the implications of the changing distribution of refugee crises and the increasingly global, but unpredictable, pattern of refugee flows (Zetter, 1999).

Concerned that the flow of refugees and asylum seekers was thus set to rise, although in reality the growth was not that dramatic, the previous Conservative government adopted increasingly restrictionist policies and statutory controls against asylum seekers and potential programme refugees – such as Bosnians. A variety of deterrent measures was instituted designed to prevent asylum seekers 'selecting' Britain as their refuge. These measures were counterbalanced by the establishment of a punitive attitude to asylum seekers who were in the country or who gained access after the new 'regime' was developed – withdrawal of basic entitlements, detention, restricted and fast-track status determination, appeal and repatriation procedures and so on. Stigmatising terminology such as 'bogus asylum seekers' and the then government's widely advertised view of widespread benefit fraud by asylum seekers accompanied the legislative changes. As a result of the changes detailed below, asylum applications dropped from 44,000 in 1995 to 29,600 in 1996 (Home Office, 1998). In that year nearly 49,000 decisions were reached, over 38,000 applicants were rejected – an increase of nearly 50% on the previous year – and only just over 2,200 accorded full refugee status, about the same figure as the previous year (UNHCR, 1997). Some 52,000 cases and 21,000 appeals were pending in 1998 at the time of the government's proposals for policy review (Home Office, 1998).

These actions also impacted on attitudes to refugees already in Britain, as well as those whose status, were they to seek entry, would never be in question. In short, Britain has been one of the leaders, among its European Union partners, in the growth of restrictionism, to the extent that the international humanitarian regime is considered to be in crisis.

The present government has reviewed policies with regard to refugees and asylum seekers. Indications from the White Paper proposals published in mid-1998, *Fairer, faster and firmer* (Home Office, 1998) and now published in the *1999 Asylum and Immigration Bill* (February 1999) are for a continuation of much of the current regime, although with concessions to asylum claimants

before the end of 1995 who will be granted Exceptional or Indefinite Leave to Remain (ELR and ILR). The main impact of the proposals will be further to accentuate demand for RSL accommodation and the supporting services of Refugee Community-based Organisations (RCOs) which has been the outcome of the 1996 legislation. But, as we indicate in Chapters 4 to 6, it is both the type of accommodation and the pattern of service providers which already give rise to current concern about the quality of service, the lack of coordination, limited institutional capacity and constrained resource base. The implications of the government's policy review are considered in more detail in Chapter 7.

Since housing is one of the basic needs and, until recently, has been recognised as one of the basic entitlements of asylum seekers and refugees, it merits research and examination in its own right. Interestingly, RSLs have not been the subject of detailed research to date. This is despite having played an active role in such provision, offering potential advantages over other providers in terms of expertise in management and support services for special needs clients like refugees and asylum seekers. However, two specific factors give research on associations a vital focus at the present time. First is their growth as the main providers of social housing in Britain – a form of provision on which this client group has always been substantially dependent. Second, and more pressing, are the recent changes in the housing benefits and welfare entitlement of asylum seekers. These changes have had a dramatic impact on the demand for RSL accommodation, while at the same time circumscribing the role of RSLs as mainstream providers for this client group.

Statutory and judicial context

The relative stability of the legal context of refugees and asylum seekers entering or already in the UK was fundamentally altered by the *1993 Asylum and Immigration Appeals Act* and, subsequently in 1996, the *Housing Act* and the *Asylum and Immigration Act*. This legislation, and appeals brought to the Courts on behalf of asylum seekers seeking to clarify their welfare rights and housing entitlements, has increased the complexity and dynamic nature of the legal context.

The purpose of this section, therefore, is to give a brief overview of the current situation within which the research was conducted, rather than a detailed legal exposition which, in any case, is likely to be overtaken by events. It should be noted that the Refugee Council provides detailed briefing and updating on the legal context.

It is important to distinguish asylum seekers from refugees and the other categories in between – those with ELR and ILR – since one of the principal impacts of recent legislation is to reinforce the differentiation of housing entitlements, among other benefits, to which these two main categories are eligible.

Refugees are individuals or households whose status under the 1951 Geneva Convention has been approved by the UK government: that is, their 'well founded fear of persecution' has been accepted. By definition they have full status to reside in the UK and have all the rights as people who are settled here. Those with full refugee status are eligible for assistance under the homelessness legislation and qualify for the housing register.

Individual refugees, as opposed to other categories of asylum seekers, have the right to reunite their families in the UK, which obviously has implications for the type of provision needed. In addition, permanent resettlement means that refugees are permitted to work. These advantages, compared with asylum seekers, mean that many refugee communities who have been resident for some time display some evidence of social and economic integration and progression through different stages of the housing supply process.

Traditionally, local authority housing departments have been the first point of access for housing by refugees and asylum seekers. The authorities were placed under an obligation to provide accommodation for those who were a priority. RSLs have also played a role. Access to employment or benefits has meant that refugee families more easily satisfy the criteria for RSL accommodation. Provision has, however, been very limited, partly because of the small overall numbers involved, the lack of leverage which individual, spontaneously arriving, refugees could exercise in terms of their

special needs, and because of the associations' need to safeguard against financial risk from rent arrears.

Large numbers of those who claim refugee status, and indeed perceive themselves to be refugees, are not necessarily granted this status by the Home Office. There are several sub-categories and the legislation provides varying degrees of constraint for each. Many claimants are granted either ELR or, slightly more secure, ILR. They are generally in the same position as refugees with regard to housing access. ELR status, applying at most to about 20% of asylum seekers, is discretionary for a year, and can be renewed for three years, whereupon full refugee status may be granted. As with refugees, those with ELR and ILR are also eligible for assistance under the homelessness legislation and qualify for the housing register. They cannot, however, reunite their families, and are thus effectively single-person households.

Asylum seekers enjoy no such certainty of access to housing or other benefits. First the *1993 Asylum and Immigration Appeals Act* introduced more discretionary rights to housing which began to "deprive asylum seekers of decent secure housing" (HACT, 1994b, p 4). Then the two 1996 statutes, the *Housing Act* and the *Asylum and Immigration Act*, defined new regulations and categories and codified disentitlements. As regards housing entitlement, asylum seekers are non-qualifying for the purposes of the housing register. However, there are exceptions to this, principally, nationals of countries which have signed agreements with the UK or EU/ EEA (eg Slovakia, Cyprus, Czech Republic, Turkey, Romania and others). It can be difficult for asylum seekers in this category to exert their right against sceptical housing officers.

With regard to other benefit entitlements (including homeless persons assistance, housing benefit, income support), the 1996 legislation made further restrictions and distinctions. Income support and housing benefit entitlement for in-country and 'on appeal' applicants were initially removed by regulation, restored by the courts and then written into the *1996 Asylum and Immigration Act*, along with housing and homelessness restrictions. Housing benefit eligibility is available to anyone on temporary admission (ie including port of entry applicants, whether or not they have had an initial refusal). It is estimated that about 4,000-5,000 families (about 20,000-25,000 people) were in this category of port-of-entry claimants in London at the end of 1997, and provided with temporary accommodation under homelessness legislation (All Party Group on Homelessness and Housing Need, 1997).

Ironically, three quarters of all successful asylum applications are made in-country (All Party Group on Homelessness and Housing Need, 1997), yet this category was disqualified from eligibility to benefits and homeless persons assistance. Support, now, is only provided as a priority under the *1989 Children Act* or the *1948 National Assistance Act* – discussed below. However, there are two further exceptions which do provide eligibility for homelessness assistance. The first is where an upheaval declaration is made by the UK government about the country of origin of an asylum seeker already in-country and who cannot safely return or be repatriated. This is restricted to new, not existing, asylum seekers whose applications have been made within the relevant times. The second category is for transitional protection for asylum seekers after 6 February 1996. From that date, only those awaiting an appeal decision, or entitled to, or in receipt of, housing benefit, or who had not received an adverse decision, were entitled to homeless persons assistance, but only until a negative decision on their application was issued.

These crude measures were intended to restrict public sector expenditure by removing access to public funds for thousands of sanctuary seekers but for whom there was no decision about their future residential status. The intention was also to provide a deterrent to would-be asylum seekers, that Britain was no longer a desirable country of refuge. These measures, which came into effect in February 1996, had a profoundly devastating impact. They drove into destitution and homelessness thousands of *asylum seekers, mainly single people by definition, who were deemed to be ineligible under Section 185(1) of the 1996 Housing Act.* To mitigate the hardship, many voluntary organisations and churches provided shelter, especially in London, where the impact of the legislation was most severe. After negative rulings by the Court of Appeal in June 1996 and the restoration of benefits, the government reintroduced these disqualifying measures in August through

Section 9 of the *1996 Asylum and Immigration Act.* This created even more chaos, intensified hardship and destitution and placed mounting pressure on hard pressed local authorities and voluntary agencies.

Subsequently, following appeals brought on behalf of asylum seekers, a ruling by the High Court in October 1996, upheld by a ruling in the Court of Appeal in February 1997, decided that local authorities had a duty to provide housing and sustenance to the homeless under Section 21 of the *1948 National Assistance Act.* There is also the (even remoter) possibility that local authorities can support people in tenancies, not just the homeless. As a result, the responsibility for homeless asylum seekers now shifted from housing departments and fell on SSDs who have had to make provision for thousands of asylum seekers. While in principle this ruling redressed some of the inequities of the legislation, of course the SSDs do not have the facilities to accommodate such large numbers of needy asylum seekers. So in practice, the problem remains. Further rulings by the High Court in May 1997 decided that local authorities had a duty to provide both food and accommodation under the 1948 Act, but cash payments were ruled ultra vires by the High Court in July 1997.

These embargoes also extended to the local authority nomination of such persons to RSLs until the emergency measures by the government in February 1998. After that date, local authorities can grant a tenancy for their stock through a third party such as RSLs; this is rather similar to the *1989 Children Act* provision discussed below.

This sequence of actions and the intensifying uncertainty brought the system, in London at least, near to collapse. The number of asylum seekers supported under the 1948 Act had grown from about 900 in late 1996 to almost 7,000 a year later. Local authorities, and even departments within the same authority, were competing with each other to find the diminishing supply of cheap Bed and Breakfast accommodation. Asylum seekers were also being put in competition with other marginal groups seeking cheap accommodation, thus increasing the stigma and rejection they faced. Because of accentuating pressures of homelessness and the burden of high costs of this accommodation on local authorities, some London boroughs started to ship asylum seekers out to lower cost locations outside the capital. This action was checked by a ruling of the High Court in December 1997 when the Medical Foundation, and others, presented compelling psychological reasons why asylum seekers should not be sent away from their communities of temporary abode. They successfully contested the 'exporting of asylum seekers' (Newham London Borough Council ex parte Medical Foundation and others) using para 3.25 of the policy guidance issued under Section 7 of the *1970 Local Authorities Social Service Act*, which requires local authorities to devise "the most cost effective package of services that meets the user's care needs, taking account of the user's and carer's own preferences". Subsequent rulings on placement outside London have been less favourable.

Asylum seekers with children have scarcely been treated less harshly by the two 1996 Acts. This category has recourse to the provisions of Sections 17 and 20 of the *1989 Children Act*. The duty falls on local authorities to provide for a child in need and to promote the welfare of children within the family. Clearly housing is a key service for the child and the family within this interpretation. Unlike those eligible for national assistance under the *1948 National Assistance Act*, those eligible for services under the 1989 Act can receive cash payments and rent payments. Also, whereas the *1996 Housing Act* prevented local housing authorities from housing asylum seekers, they can make available properties to SSDs to fulfil their duties under the 1989 Act. This may be achieved either directly or indirectly through a third party such as an RSL which could manage the properties. This would be a cheaper option than Bed and Breakfast. In practice, the bureaucratic complexity of this tripartite procedure, especially outside unitary authorities, has again militated against this possibility. Despite this, our study has found some examples of the practice. Inevitably there is concern that it is the hard to let and void properties that will be made available under these provisions. Indications are that provision under the 1989 Act, in London alone, rose from about 700 families in late 1996 to nearly 4,500 families (10,000 people) a year later (All Party Working Group on Homelessness and Housing Need, 1997).

Paradoxically, the effect of the legislative and judicial yo-yo has been to draw many thousands more people into the dependency net. Perhaps the group worst affected by the loss of emergency and other rented accommodation were actually the asylum seekers who applied on entry and were entitled to benefits. The increased dependency is especially ironic since there is countless research evidence to show that refugees and asylum seekers are among the most industrious and self-sufficient members of a community. In the past, the vast majority of asylum seekers would have obtained accommodation in the private rented sector with the aid of housing benefit. This enabled a degree of choice and independence about where to live. However, forced into destitution without benefit or income, they are now totally dependent on SSD assistance. Uncertainty over asylum seeker benefits, together with the general problems created by cutting housing benefit for young single people, has now made it almost impossible to place asylum seekers and even refugees in the private rented sector. Thus the impact of demand switches is likely to increase pressure on RSL stock.

The main effect, of course, has been to switch the costs of supporting asylum seekers from the central government funded benefits system to local authorities' revenue income. While a proportion of the maximum £165 per week (though in practice much less) 'payment' to individual asylum seekers is recoverable through Home Office grants, local General Funds have borne unplanned high levels of expenditure. The overall cost to the public purse, far from being reduced as originally intended, has risen significantly, with *1948 National Assistance Act* provision costing in excess of £3,000 pa per asylum seeker in receipt of benefit. The Association of London Government assessed the cost of preventing widespread destitution among asylum seekers at £40m pa, while some estimates put the total cost to London boroughs alone of £120m in 1997.

Equally disturbing, these events have, probably intentionally, increased the competition between asylum seekers and other low income, marginal and impoverished groups for scarce resources. By virtue of being mainly single, many asylum seekers are concentrated by being accommodated in hostels. This does little to ease potential conflict between them and local communities. Community relations have been damaged and the increased community tensions do little to help already traumatised forced migrants from rebuilding their shattered lives.

The impact on RSLs

Asylum seekers have been progressively squeezed out of local authority provided social housing – both direct and indirect provision – by the two 1996 Acts. Non-qualifying asylum seekers cannot be allocated council tenancies or homelessness assistance. Denial of access has thus intensified pressures on the other main source of social housing – RSLs. What have been the implications?

For both refugees and asylum seekers, as our study shows, RSLs are well placed to provide accommodation, although in practice few do and quality is variable. But the legal uncertainty of the last few years makes the offer of housing both complicated and risky.

With regard to **refugees**, the situation remains unchanged. RSLs can continue to provide for this category, subject to their normal letting policies and criteria. As our study shows, while a number of them have accommodated refugees in the past and still do so today, provision is very small scale and, by and large, not tailored to the specialist needs of this tenant group.

So far as provision for **asylum seekers** is concerned, the picture for RSLs is radically different and rather more complex, as the review of legislative and judicial context has implied. Indeed this review has been necessary, not only because it illustrates a major theme of our study – RSL practice and provision cannot be separated from the wider context of structural factors and conditions. More particularly, it indicates some of the reasons why RSLs – even those committed to serving the interests of this tenant group –have been constrained by a very cautious response to obvious needs.

As already noted, under two limited conditions, following the emergency provisions of February 1998 and the *1986 Children Act*, RSLs can act as a third party to manage local authority stock for non-qualifying asylum seekers.

However, the outright bans applying to local authorities accommodating asylum seekers have never directly applied to RSLs. They have the discretion to decide to whom they wish to offer housing.

Salient here are two Housing Corporation Circulars, Circular *R3 – 04/97*, 'Lettings to certain persons [from] abroad' (January 1997) and Circular *R3 – 34/97*, 'Temporary lettings to asylum seekers' (January 1998). These circulars summarised the legislative implications for RSLs, of the two 1996 Acts and the principal judicial decisions made under the *1948 National Assistance Act* and the *1989 Children Act*. The first circular, while noting the ban on local authorities making housing provision for asylum seekers, recognised that "RSLs are independent bodies – some of whom have aims and objectives which include the provision of housing to [asylum seekers]" (Housing Corporation Circular *R3 04/97*, para 2.7). However, the circular warned that if RSLs were to consider applications from asylum seekers they would need to consider carefully:

- whether their aims and objectives allowed them to accommodate asylum seekers;

- whether provision contravened the normal lettings policy of making available permanent accommodation when by implication the non-qualifying asylum seekers might not be considered permanent;

- the financial effect of housing asylum seekers who might not have the means to pay rents and service charges.

Not surprisingly, the effect of this circular was to increase the overall caution with which RSLs considered asylum seeker applications. It reinforced the reluctance of those RSLs which were already unwilling to consider this group. For those RSLs who were more disposed to house asylum seekers, procedures were reviewed, often by the board, to minimise the risks. In some cases, numerical limit were set to the number of tenancies to be provided to asylum seekers. As our study shows, it was mainly the smaller, community-based RSLs which were generally more responsive to the crisis. Assessment procedures for these applicants were tightened up; applicants were very carefully assessed as to their benefits entitlements, with the assistance of specialist agencies and community workers. Nonetheless, the level of housing need was usually a crucial criterion for RSLs who did consider asylum seekers. Charitable and voluntary sector agencies were approached as a source of rental cost recovery for non-entitled but needy asylum seekers. Those clearly ineligible were referred on, while the cases of those considered eligible were usually referred up to directorate level and sometimes the board. Careful monitoring of rental payments ensued, although the more sympathetic RSLs did not appear to adopt other than normal procedures for all tenants against those who might fall into arrears.

At this time, some of the more sympathetic RSLs began to explore other initiatives (London Federation of Housing Associations, 1996). These were very ad hoc and anticipated the impact of the 1996 legislation. They did not lead to concerted action, but included partnerships with charitable organisations and with SSDs in order to make accommodation available for those in greatest need but at minimum risk; hostel accommodation; hardship funds; and greater coordination between RSLs to provide dispersed short life accommodation. Our study reports on some of these partnerships.

The Housing Corporation's second circular *R3 – 34/97* supplemented the earlier circular with somewhat more encouraging guidance to RSLs. Recognising the impact of Courts' decisions on various appeal cases, the Corporation advised RSLs that:

- a small proportion of lettings from their long-term stock for local authority nominees can be made available for temporary letting to asylum seeker referrals, provided the applicant comes within the terms of Part VII of the *1996 Housing Act* or the *1948 National Assistance Act* or the *1989 Children Act*; the letting is an assured shorthold tenancy;

- any lettings to asylum seekers under these terms need (a) the written agreement of the housing authority and (b) the RSL's board agreement that the aims and objectives were being met;

- tenancies under these conditions can continue until all appeal routes have been exhausted; and even then, advising that duty may then be owed under the *1948 National Assistance Act* or the

1989 Children Act;

- RSLs should make arrangements with SSDs for the payment of rent and service costs where provision is made under the *1948 National Assistance Act* or the *1989 Children Act*;

- provision under these conditions are not recorded as nominations in CORE.

However,

- such lettings are likely to affect grant recovery rules, obliging RSLs to repay capital grant for change of use of property when, assuming there are no further changes, the Corporation carries out a review in two years' time.

Despite the implied penalty in the last clause, reading between the lines, the overall tenor of the circular is reasonably positive. The guidance is quite encouraging in terms of promoting the need for arrangements with SSDs; and it implies support for tenants in acknowledging the potentially protracted nature of appeals. Nonetheless, while relaxing somewhat guidance in the earlier circular, the net effect on RSL activity remains modest. By and large RSLs may be more comfortable in developing partnerships with local authorities. But the scope of activity and provision has not, as yet, dramatically increased.

Related research and literature survey

Constituting a relatively small but distinctive social group in the UK, refugees and asylum seekers have attracted relatively little research interest until recently. Apart from the stimulus created by the arrival of programme or quota refugees, such as Ugandan Asians and Vietnamese, and given the extensive research conducted on other socially excluded or marginalised groups, the lack of a substantive body of research is all the more surprising. In comparison, for example, with Europe, particularly the Nordic countries and the USA, UK-based research into the characteristics of this group has been somewhat partial and very fragmented. Moreover, the focus is almost wholly on refugees or those with reasonably secure status, not asylum seekers.

Restrictionist policies towards refugee and asylum

seekers, cynically linked to immigration control policies on the one hand, and the increasing global attention given to refugee emergencies on the other, have dramatically raised the political profile of this group in the last four years or so. This has only served to highlight the research vacuum in this field. Lacking a longitudinal perspective and overall pattern of findings compounds the difficulties of building up a more detailed understanding of the diversity and comparative characteristics of this group. It also limits the extent to which research can effectively inform policy.

Housing research

With a limited tradition of independently funded academic inquiry, UK research on refugee resettlement in general and refugee housing issues in particular, is strongly policy responsive. This is somewhat ironic given that successive UK governments have (deliberately?) failed to build public sector institutional structures, or defined reception and resettlement policies or resources for refugees arriving from different regions of the world (Majke, 1991; RC, 1997a). In contrast to countries such as the USA (Majke, 1991) and the Netherlands (RC, 1997), and in the absence of specific policies and programmes, UK government responses have been characteristically pragmatic, laissez-faire, front-loaded to reception stages and uncoordinated between the mass of agencies to whom the provider responsibility falls (Quiglan, 1993). Benign neglect contrasts with the vigour with which governments have sought to limit the call on public resources, at least at the national level. The corollary has been to impose a reliance on non-governmental institutions and resources from the voluntary and community sectors to provide for the needs of refugees and asylum seekers.

Accordingly, research into resettlement policies and the role of providers supporting that process, parallels this experience. What research has been conducted has tended to focus on non-governmental agencies and community-based organisations and their interaction with statutory providers such as local authorities and RSLs. It is the literature relating to these themes which provides the main entry point for our own study.

Housing need and provision are consistently

identified in much of the generically-based research literature on the refugee and asylum seeker population, as a crucial element in refugee reception and settlement experiences (see for example, Field, 1985; AMA, 1991; Robinson, 1993a; Carey Wood et al, 1995). These generic studies have informed our own work. Yet there has been little systematic research specifically on refugees and housing beyond some operational needs (for example, HACT, 1994a; 1994b). Our study aims to tackle this shortfall, although limited to one, albeit increasingly important, provider of housing for this client group.

Policy-driven research: refugee settlement and housing

Given the policy-driven nature of research in this field, applied investigation and operational requirements predominate. Exploration of social needs and social policy issues, together with assessment of the institutional framework and the role of providers, community support agencies, networks and partnerships, comprise the primary focus of research. Commissioned studies form the majority of the work.

Many of the existing studies have been commissioned or conducted by voluntary organisations. Essential though they are, in setting the context of the present study, a point of caution is needed. These tend to highlight the more contentious and sensitive aspects of refugees' experience of resettlement and the problems faced by non-statutory providers. Thus, some of the recent documents, highlighting the crisis provoked by the *1996 Asylum and Immigration Act* and the *1996 Housing Act*, are referred to, not necessarily as evidence, but in so far as they enrich our awareness of the highly charged political context within which our own study is located.

In relation to housing-specific findings, there are many points of contact with the present study. Many of the generic findings about the resettlement experiences of refugees and asylum seekers and the role played by service providers in this process, merit further investigation and testing in the context of RSLs. Among the important issues we have identified relevant to our own study are the following.

The study closest to our own, *Housing issues facing refugee communities in London*, was conducted in 1994 (HACT, 1994b). The role of RCOs, including their relationship to RSLs, and the attempts by RCOs to establish themselves as RSLs, are significant themes which our own research picks up. The study revealed the precarious and constrained existence of RCOs and the inaccessibility of mainstream housing provision (local authorities and RSLs) to them. Overall, the study paints a bleak picture for the future, both for RCOs as agencies providing the specialist support for and understanding of this unique client group, and also more generally, for the clients themselves, where the prognosis was for continuing acute and largely unmet need (HACT, 1994b, p 11). Our own study takes up these themes in order to shed more light on the need for, and form of partnerships and coordination between different service providers in the housing field – one of the recommendations of the HACT study. Significantly, this study concluded that "most groups [ie RCOs], felt that their best hope of providing housing for their communities was in partnership with larger housing associations" (HACT, 1994b, p 14). This contention provides one of several important entry points for our own study. The HACT report did not interview refugees according to a standard questionnaire and through a sample frame. The present study does. Direct insight into the refugees' and asylum seekers' own experiences and perceptions will enrich our understanding of the issues.

An early British Refugee Council report, *Settling for a future* (BRC, 1987) noted, among other conclusions, the importance of a coordinated approach between local authorities, RSLs, the voluntary sector and RCOs. A perceived need for reception centres was also identified. While a decade later circumstances have changed completely, both these conclusions are mirrored in the orientation of our own study. Coordination of the different agencies and the complementary skills and resources they contribute to housing provision for this group still remains problematic. The need for properly resourced reception centres is more pressing than ever, given the rise in asylum seekers over the last decade, their statutory exclusion from more conventional provision by virtue of the 1996 Act, and the growing proportion of whom have uncertain status.

The deficiency in provision of reception centres, where refugees and asylum seekers may be left to fend for themselves, is also identified by another recent study (Refugee Housing Association, 1997). Because it focuses on an issue high on the UK refugee policy agenda and one closely connected to housing provision, the scope of this report is especially relevant to the current research study. Except for quota refugees, the UK has no coordinated reception policy. As another HACT study points out (1994a), reception centres have only been used for quota refugees. Provision for spontaneous arrivals, especially at the present time, is ad hoc; but both RSLs and semi-registered social landlords are significant providers of hostel accommodation which effectively substitutes for properly constituted reception centres. Variation in reception centre policy and practice in a number of European countries is identified in the report. Problems of social isolation, marginalisation from the mainstream of social life and the potentially burdensome constraints and obligations of reception centre regimes are recorded. These are important conclusions which form the backdrop to our own research and findings on hostels/reception centres.

Another document by the BRC, *Working together* (BRC, 1988), gave early recognition to the significance of RCOs in providing services to refugees; the report re-emphasised the 1987 report's call for partnership between the various actors. Produced under very different circumstances than today, the report, nevertheless, anticipates some of the key issues raised in the recent Refugee Council policy document, *The development of a refugee settlement policy in the UK* (RC, 1997a), in which housing provision and reception centres are again identified as key elements in a humane and responsive refugee settlement policy. From the line of analysis pursued in this report, and in the specific circumstances of the impact of recent housing and asylum seeker legislation, the Refugee Council appears a firm advocate of reception centre provision.

The most extensive and most systematic of the generic research projects conducted about refugees is that commissioned by the Home Office in 1995 (Carey Wood et al, 1995). This sector-by-sector review contains a chapter on housing context, type of accommodation, tenure, mobility and so on.

Interestingly, this is the longest chapter in the study, and although only an overview, contains the significant comment that there may be poor knowledge of RSL provision on the part of refugees and that their perceptions may have been blurred by the negative experiences of some already in RSL accommodation (Carey Wood et al, 1995, p 68). This observation is significant in terms of the potential uptake of RSL property, given the reliance which new arrivals place on the information and experience provided by the network of family, friends and community groups already resident (Carey Wood et al, 1995, p 67). Although, over time, information from public bodies substitutes for experiential information, the fact that refugee needs are likely to be more acute on arrival than after some adaptation has taken place, suggests that early impressions may influence housing choices later on.

Our own research picks up some of this ambivalence which refugees and asylum seekers displayed toward RSLs in this earlier study. It is reflected in the tension we have identified between the RCOs, with their claim to offer specialist insights into the specific context and needs of this client group, and the generally better resourced general needs RSLs who are the main providers.

Echoing both the findings of another Home Office study a decade earlier (Field, 1985) and Robinson's independent observation (Robinson, 1993a) that housing provision for refugees should be set within the wider context of resettlement policies, one very significant conclusion of the 1995 study is that good housing is as important as economic well-being for contributing to a sense of their being part of the community (Robinson, 1993a, p 96). The implied relationship in this statement, between housing provision and the wider framework of community-based support for which agencies like RSLs have some responsibility to provide, is a central theme of our study.

A HACT study (HACT, 1994a) investigating refugee housing needs in the North, was one of the first to observe the effects of the *1993 Asylum and Immigration Appeals Act* which, by severely constraining asylum seeker access to housing, provoked the crisis of the last four years. This report highlights the distinctive background of asylum seekers and refugees and the impact this has

on their requirements for basic needs such as housing. Further, the importance of differentiating the needs of asylum seekers and refugees, those that are new arrivals as compared to those who are settled with more established networks and support, is emphasised. Attention is also drawn to the unequal access to housing experienced by this population, a feature shared with ethnic minorities generally. The poorer quality accommodation which this group invariably occupies is also documented. These are all pointers to issues surrounding housing process and provision which our own study explores in more detail.

Interestingly, the majority of respondents in this study found RSLs helpful, especially in relation to speed of offer, quality of property, service and maintenance. Conversely, negative responses mainly related to the access process – waiting lists, offers, etc. This apparent polarity suggests considerable variation in experiences which might be explained by the inevitably small and unrepresentative sample which is a feature of much refugee research. Equally, it also indicates that refugees and asylum seekers do discern the considerable variation in the practices and procedures of RSLs and other housing agencies – an important feature which our study confirms. Our own study confirms these findings.

Three regionally-based studies indicate additional matters for investigation. The main findings of the HACT study (1994b) have already been discussed. Robinson's survey of service providers for refugees in Wales (Robinson, 1999), while not a study of housing provision per se, provides findings which are very relevant to our own investigation of the housing sector. He concludes that there are low levels of consultation by service providers with refugee groups; that services are not targeted to refugees; and that the lack of awareness of refugees allows them to be sidelined in policy making. Although his conclusions only endorse many of the outcomes of the earlier generic research, their value is in confirming that refugee marginalisation remains a persistent characteristic of service provision. Our own research frame was designed to reveal the extent to which similar experiences of marginalisation and poor targeting apply in the specific field of RSL provision and the implications this has for developing best practice.

A recent study of resettlement processes and providers in Cambridge draws attention to three issues in relation to housing processes (Humm, 1996). The study indicates that there is a lack of an overall strategy with regard to housing provision for refugees and asylum seekers. As a consequence, the study also observes that there is a very limited range of choice available to this client group. Third, the study endorses the well-established view that the needs of this client group change over time. These three issues merit further investigation in the context of RSL provision.

Programme or quota refugee research

Another theme of academic research comprises largely critical post mortems on programme refugee resettlement policies, such as for Ugandan Asians (Robinson, 1985; 1993b), Vietnamese (Duke and Marshall, 1995) and Chileans (Joly, 1996). Apart from reinforcing the conclusions from generic studies about the role of key housing variables – tenure, location access, quality and so on – drawing generic conclusions from ethnic specific research is difficult.

Relevant to the present study, however, these earlier studies show how the combination of the then fashionable dispersal policies and insufficient coordination in the provision of housing resources led to significant policy failure. These shortcomings were replicated in each case of programme refugees. Although the objective of dispersal was to dilute impacts, paradoxically it accentuated secondary migration (always a characteristic of refugee settlement processes), and the spatial concentration of refugee communities. Robinson suggests that reliance on voluntary offers of local authority housing was also a major flaw (Robinson, 1985). The resulting lack of housing prompted the Ugandan Asians to act on their own and seek housing in areas of already high ethnic concentration.

Joly (1996) confirms Robinson's analysis (1993a, 1993b) against dispersal and argues for some degree of clustering, not only because of its inevitability, but more positively because, if effectively organised, it can encourage community formation and self-sufficiency. Anticipating these findings, Field (1985) also argues against the policy of dispersed

resettlement utilised for Chilean and Vietnamese refugees. A cautionary note is sounded in this study about the more favoured clustering approach: allocation of housing, where there is heavily localised demand, can create problematic outcomes for the provider as well as for the refugees.

In conclusion, although there are many contrasts with the focus of current policy and research, the housing aspects of programme refugee research highlight three significant aspects which our own research follows up: the importance of secondary migration to the demand for housing; the problematic reliance on voluntary housing supply even where this is provided by socially oriented agencies; and the importance of community clustering in supporting the settlement and integration of refugees and asylum seekers.

Appendix B: Perceptions and experiences of refugees and asylum seekers in RSL property

Introduction

A major objective of our study was to assess the scope of housing provision and the range of management practices of RSLs from the perspective of the beneficiaries – the refugees and asylum seekers. We interviewed a sample of 46 RSL tenants which was further supplemented by a small number of 'group' interviews, for example, with a Somali women's group, and data collected from representatives of community organisations (RCOs). The primary aim of this part of the research was to draw into our understanding of RSL provision and practice the experiences of refugee and asylum seeker tenants.

Characteristics of the sample

The nationality of those interviewed is contained in Table B1. It can be seen from this that Somalis and Tamils are the major groups in the sample, reflecting their concentration in Tower Hamlets and Newham. Eastern Europeans, including Albanians, Bosnians, a Romanian and Yugoslav, are next in numerical significance. Other African groups are represented by Sudan and Rwanda, and the Middle East by Israel and Kurdistan (Iran). The isolated example of a Chilean couple from the 1970s is also included as a point of comparison with later refugee groups.

Table B1: Nationality of respondents

Nationality	Number of respondents	Percentage
Albanian	3	7
Bosnian	5	11
Chilean	1	2
Israeli	1	2
Kurdish	1	2
Romanian	1	2
Rwandan	2	4
Somali	15	33
Sudanese	6	13
Tamil	10	22
Yugoslav	1	?
Total	46	100

An attempt was made to draw up a sample in which the refugee status of respondents is fairly evenly balanced between asylum seekers and those with Exceptional Leave to Remain (ELR) (see Table B2). Full refugee status was confined to those groups who had longer periods of stay in the UK, specifically Somalis and the one Chilean in the sample. The temporary protection category refers to the special status given to Bosnian refugees under the terms of the Bosnian Programme. Given that the greatest immediate pressure on housing resources is from those groups without full refugee status, the focus on this category seemed appropriate. Of note is the fact that it was also harder to identify full status refugees since many RSLs did not differentiate the residential/immigration status of their tenants.

Table B2: Refugee status of respondents

Status	Number of respondents	Percentage
Asylum seeker	15	33
Exceptional Leave to Remain	19	41
Full refugee status	6	13
Temporary protection	5	11
On appeal	1	2
Total	46	100

It can be seen that the bulk of respondents, some 80%, were either in receipt of benefits or if disallowed benefits under the *1996 Asylum and Immigration Act* were provided for under the *1948 National Assistance Act* (Table B3). Again, this reflects the fact that the sample is biased towards more recent arrivals, those less likely to be settled and in employment.

Table B3: Employment status of respondents

Status	Number of respondents	Percentage
Full time	4	9
Temp work	1	2
On benefits	30	65
Student	3	7
Social services	7	15
Other	1	2
Total	46	100

In terms of household characteristics, there were 25 single households in the sample (54%), 15 single parent households with children (33%), four couples with children (9%) and two couples without children (4%). Of the 25 single households 18 were young people (ages 18-35) and seven elderly (60 and above). Young, single people therefore represent 39% of the total sample. Many of these have arrived recently (one half had arrived in Britain less than two years from the date of interview) and over one half are asylum seekers, with little or no community support in their areas of residence. Of the significant number of single parent households (one third of the sample) only one was male-headed, while the vast majority were Somali women with children whose husbands had either been killed or were in camps in Ethiopia or Kenya. In this respect,

a distinctive feature of the two London boroughs in the sample is the position of female-headed households in the Somali population (AMA, 1991, cited in Robinson, 1999; El-Sohl, 1991; Bloch, 1996). The special needs of this group are developed in the discussion in Chapter 4. Elderly people are another distinctive group (22% of the total sample) whose needs and characteristics are also addressed in more detail. The diversity of need present within refugee populations is, however, often overlooked within the process of bureaucratic labelling (Robinson, 1999).

While a comparatively small and not a fully representative sample of the different groups of refugees and asylum seekers, an obvious, but nonetheless important characteristic which these data endorse, is the great diversity of refugee and asylum seeker communities – status, ethnic/national origin, levels of self-sufficiency and household structure. As our data and earlier discussion in Chapter 2 imply, refugees/asylum seeker status imposes complex social, economic and legal burdens on the households. This is compounded by the fact that the household composition is likely to display unusual characteristics – separated families, single persons, and so on, as our data indicate.

These preliminary characteristics, revealed in this sample, have significant implications for RSLs' policy and practice. This diversity should be reflected in the type of accommodation and support services which RSLs should expect to provide and the quality of service delivery which these tenants could be entitled to expect.

As our examination of RSLs in the next two chapters reveals, the extremely variable standards of response and the lack of specific provision tailored to the needs of particular refugee and asylum seeker groups indicate a very limited appreciation of this diversity of need. Bad practice is, thankfully, not widespread, at least in the experience of the respondents. But there are already clear indicators of the need substantially to improve and sensitise existing practice. These are reinforced in subsequent sections.

Geographical location and the significance of community groups

Table B.4 demonstrates the distribution of respondents. In the present sample, Somalis and Tamils are the principal nationalities in the two London boroughs selected to be case study areas – Tower Hamlets and Newham. The geographical spread reflects to a large extent the distribution of the refugee asylum seeker population as a whole. As the Home Office study (Carey-Wood et al, 1995, p 15) had indicated, over 80% of refugees in Britain are concentrated in the Greater London area. The majority of the sample in this study is in London, which reflects the level of housing demand in the capital. Our sample, however, is located in two London boroughs, selected because of our initial contacts with and knowledge of RSL and community groups in these localities. Manchester, on the other hand, which was added to our survey later on, has a small number of respondents.

Housing history

Eighteen, or 39% of the respondents, had moved to their present area to take up accommodation and 13 (28%) to be closer to family or friends. These were the two main reasons for living in their present area, although this was more pronounced in the London boroughs in the sample. Although it is difficult to generalise given the limited size of the sample, a clear distinction can be drawn between case study areas.

In the London boroughs, the majority of individuals had located in order to be near family and relatives or to take up accommodation. This is in contrast to Birmingham, where two out of 12 respondents had been referred by the Refugee Arrivals Project and another four had arrived in the area through convoys organised under the Bosnia Programme. An additional three Albanians had arrived in Birmingham by chance and had been referred to the Midland Refugee Council by the police. The presence of settled communities in the two London boroughs in the sample may be a contributory factor in explaining movement into the areas in contrast to Birmingham where outside referral was the norm.

The implication of these findings is that, so far as London is concerned, the desire to regroup in co-ethnic communities appears to be a significant characteristic in the housing process. This corroborates earlier research which has noted that most refugees and asylum seekers, in the past, have countered UK government dispersal policies with secondary migration in order to create homogenous communities.

Another significant factor in housing history is the way in which accommodation was obtained by those in the sample. The findings of the North East study (HACT, 1994a) are confirmed in the present study, in that 22 of the respondents (48%) had found their present accommodation through friends and relatives.

Given the evidence of secondary migration documented in this and earlier research, these findings on housing history indicate that a potentially strong motivating factor influencing the pattern and destination of secondary migration is the availability of housing – in this case RSL property. This has implications for the scale of provision which RSLs, already engaged in accommodating refugees and asylum seekers, may be called upon to recognise in the future.

Table B.4 Location of respondents

Location	Number of respondents	Percentage
Birmingham	12	26
Manchester	6	13
London boroughs		
Newham	15	33
Tower Hamlets	13	28
Total	46	100

Experience of current RSL accommodation

Twenty-two respondents, or 48% of the sample, were living in flats, 11 shared houses, another 11 lived in hostels (three in rooms and eight in bedsits) and two were in a reception centre in Birmingham (Refugee Housing Association).

Access and allocation

The main issue in relation to obtaining accommodation was the **length of time respondents had to wait to be housed**. Fourteen respondents complained of problems in this respect (30% of the sample). *A minority had waited for up to three years to find accommodation!* This again confirms the findings of the North East study, where the author remarks that "negative comments about housing associations ... tended to focus on difficulties in gaining access to accommodation" (HACT, 1994a, p 12).

The survey also highlighted other aspects of **the access and allocation processes**. In a few cases the points system operated by some RSLs was seen as arbitrary and open to manipulation by housing managers. Allocation of housing was seen *in these cases at least* as overly bureaucratic and unfair in its effects. A common expression used by tenants concerned the lack of suitable accommodation: "what was offered was not *suitable*", as several of them explained. A related issue, voiced by both housing managers and tenants, was that an 'only-one-offer' policy effectively forced tenants to take up accommodation which did not meet their requirements. As discussed below, from the viewpoint of refugees and refugee community organisations, there would appear to be a lack of accommodation which meets their specific cultural and family needs.

While it is not possible to gauge the extent to which these findings are unique to the study group, as opposed to other minority group RSL tenants, these experiences do accentuate the already high levels of vulnerability which characterise this group. This emphasises the need for enhanced sensitivity in access and allocation procedures by RSLs.

Problems with accommodation

Nearly half of the sample (43%) had experienced **problems with their accommodation** at some point, with repairs and overcrowding forming the most common complaints. In three cases individuals had raised issues of insufficient security in their accommodation, racial harassment and poor attitudes of support staff towards tenants. Of the 20 tenants who had experienced problems, six found

their landlord's response very helpful, three quite helpful, two helpful, seven unhelpful and two very unhelpful. The majority of those who found their landlords very helpful were either in refugee community RSLs or recently arrived asylum seekers with close personal relations with support staff. This suggests that *many tenants valued the type of contact with landlords or support staff with either cultural affinity or a sense of belonging provided.* Although not a statistically robust sample, a possibly significant pointer is that of the unhelpful/very unhelpful category all were from tenants in mainstream RSL properties.

This conclusion is endorsed in the next chapter; as we show there, refugee communities often possess a range of resources well attuned to their needs such as housing and which, though sometimes difficult to engage, are often underutilised by RSLs. To be fair, as pointed out in the previous chapter, some RSLs recognise that more could be done to draw on this resource, while others have not give sufficient recognition to the particular needs of this group or the resources that are able to provide. Good practice, elaborated in Chapter 6, illustrates how better engagement of refugee and asylum seeker community resources and innovative partnerships can be mutually beneficial.

In discussion with tenants, *issues of bureaucracy, delays in repairs and autocratic managerial styles were the most common sources of tension.* Amplifying an example of these problems indicates the scope of specialist needs and support which refugees and asylum seekers require from RSLs. One outreach worker for a Somali women's health project remarked on the difficulties she had faced when taken to court by an RSL in Newham over a mistaken case of rent arrears. Although this was finally resolved by the RSL sending a written apology, she pointed out that many of her clients would have been unfamiliar with the legal processes involved. Due to her excellent English she was able to contact a solicitor and have the problem resolved, but "what about people who don't know their rights?" she asked. While Somali women's groups provide a much-needed means of support, many of the women interviewed complained of social isolation and a lack of familiarity with complaints procedures in RSLs, which the above example raises.

More generally among the sample, several young women in hostels noted the difficulties in sharing with men, some of whom they regarded as "untidy", "dirty" or prone to violence. The evidence presented here indicates that women refugees, although a minority of principal asylum applicants in Britain, are "both an important group in their own right and also have distinct needs" (Robinson, 1999, p 14).

Another aspect of concern among Somali women is that, as single women and therefore the sole providers for households, many of them were aware of the difficulties in coming off benefits, balancing the need for childcare with part-time work while at the same time earning enough to pay the often high rents in those RSLs which provided additional support for tenants. In this respect many single women regarded rents as too high to meet out of their own earnings, thus reinforcing a condition of dependency on benefits which many were eager to escape from. Since this is an outcome of structural failures in the benefits system, not unique to Somali women, it is reasonable to assume that other groups would also have had these experiences of the 'poverty trap'. Given that refugees and asylum seekers are particularly vulnerable to accusations of dependency, it bears on wider RSL policy issues about the financial risks they are prepared to take and the pressures to sustain a guaranteed income stream from their tenants.

This evidence points to the need for good practice to deliver improved management systems to handle problems with accommodation, provide information and advice, review financial practices and ensure that there are effective procedures to handle complaints. Best practice in these areas must be targeted specifically to refugees and asylum seekers and sensitive to the cultural and gender issues which are of concern to them.

It needs to be stressed that **the survey found that over one half of the sample had no problems with their accommodation**. While, on the other hand, only 16 of the respondents explicitly replied to the question **on aspects they valued most in their accommodation, the responses indicate that social factors including privacy (five respondents), the provision of cultural and social activities (three respondents) and**

friendly staff (three respondents) were the most significant. When asked about which additional services they would most like to be provided by RSLs, 14 out of 21 respondents indicated social and cultural events or activities.

Social isolation

Overcoming social isolation was one of the most significant factors in the experience of the respondents. Clearly this is part of, and compounds, the more general experience of social exclusion experienced by refugees and asylum seekers. Thus, while not explicitly a factor directly related to RSL accommodation, to the extent that RSLs claim to cater for minority groups who are often marginalised, this experience deserves further investigation. Some indication of the unusual demographic structure and special needs of refugee and asylum seekers households has already been given above.

Elderly refugees are particularly vulnerable to the effects of isolation: "in our case, we are lonely", said one elderly Tamil woman living in a sheltered scheme in Newham. The main source of complaint among these elderly Tamil women, perhaps trivial to an outsider, was the restriction which was currently being placed on parking rights for their relatives. Keeping in touch with relatives was a key priority for these elderly women. Although they valued their independence, there was a constant need to overcome isolation. In this respect, most of those interviewed placed great store on the social events organised by their RSLs and regarded this as amongst the best aspects of their accommodation.

Similar issues were raised by elderly Somali refugees in a housing scheme on the Isle of Dogs, who found themselves at some distance from the bulk of the Somali community concentrated in Bethnal Green and Poplar. Isolation from the core community also affected a Chilean couple in Manchester who were stranded on a 'problem estate'. Adding to the sense of isolation was the fact that many of their co-patriots had repatriated during the 1980s.

In general, elderly refugees would often have few or no relatives remaining in their home countries to which they could return. To this is added a growing sense of alienation from what remained of the community living in exile. Young people, for example, often move away from established communities, as in the case of elderly Polish refugees in Manchester, many of whose children had migrated to London in pursuit of work. Summarising the issues faced by elderly refugees, Robinson (1999, p 14) argues, "the psychiatric scars of refugeehood can remain with an individual to death, and may even become more acute in old age".

Somali women's groups point to the array of problems faced by Somali women, including high levels of illiteracy in Somali and heightened difficulties in learning English, a lack of familiarity with welfare systems, distance from extended family networks as forms of support and the consequent effects of social isolation.

Thus, over and above the marginality of many minority groups, the specific social and personal experiences of forced migrants – family separation, loss of homeland, life long memories of trauma – highlight the sensitivity which is needed in supporting refugees and asylum seekers. These factors underline the obligation on RSLs to develop policies and practices to resource the unique social and cultural experiences and situations which these tenants confront in order to combat isolation and exclusion. Elderly refugees require additional support mechanisms which should be recognised and resourced. And for all the gender/age etc sub-groups, organised social events and proximity to co-ethnics are clearly significant needs.

Overall then, while reassuringly there is little evidence of bad practice, there are a number of key pointers to the ways in which RSLs can develop more responsive and sensitive policies and management structures with regard to this tenant group.

Levels of participation

An important part of the research was concerned with whether tenants felt that they have a say in the running of their accommodation. Thirty (65%) out of the 46 respondents were aware of regular tenants' meetings. Out of this 30, 19 had attended in the past

(41% of the total sample). Of the 11 failing to attend, four gave lack of interest as their main reason, three mentioned work commitments, two lack of information and in only one case was an "unfriendly management" given as a reason for not participating. Thirteen out of the 19 attending found the meetings very successful, four fairly successful and two unsuccessful. Reasons given for the lack of success in meetings varied from a perception of tokenism on the part of management – "they make the final decisions" as one asylum seeker remarked – to inactivity and conflict among tenants themselves. In one instance it was remarked that different national groupings will tend to "stick together", with language and ethnic differences preventing "people getting together".

Although the high success rate of meetings may be attributable to a degree of self-selection of the participants, where it did occur it was commonly associated with a general feeling of satisfaction with accommodation. As indicated earlier, tenants' perceptions of the best features of their accommodation tended to be related to social factors, such as respect for tenants' privacy, provision of social and cultural activities and friendly staff–tenant relations. In this instance, high levels of participation in meetings and successful outcomes may be positively related to tenants' perceptions of *already* feeling included in the running of their RSLs.

It is important to stress that the survey concentrated on participation in formal meetings, rather than investigating the more complex issue of empowerment. Nevertheless, there is some positive evidence that some RSLs recognise the importance of participation by refugee tenants and adopt measures to facilitate this.

The obvious requirement is for RSLs to enhance ways of working with their refugee and asylum seeker tenants which encourage participation and involvement by as large a number of this client group as possible. How non-participants can best be encouraged, individually or in groups, to become more involved in the running of their accommodation, is clearly a major priority. Our evidence suggests that social and cultural events and a sensitivity to particular ethnic or cultural factors, such as own language documents, are positive factors which stimulate participation and involvement in the residential community. Investigating the extent to which other aspects of the management experience (for example, issues of rent collection, repairs procedures), condition the willingness to participate, is also important.

Changing housing needs

In relation to how tenants would most like to see **improvements in the future performance of their RSL**, 10 out of 27 respondents indicated greater participation and cooperation between tenants as the most significant factors. This response bears out the conclusions in the previous section, that a sense of integration and control over one's environment is one of the principle factors in the perception of well-being among refugee and asylum seeker tenants.

Other factors included:

- the provision of more information
- own language materials
- reduction in waiting lists
- the encouragement of better staff–tenant relationships.

In hostels in particular there was a perceived need for greater independence, for example, a lifting of restrictions on visiting times and the provision of social and cultural events to overcome the effects of isolation.

Conclusions and summary

While acknowledging the limitations of the small sample, there are, nevertheless, significant pointers here which indicate how RSLs can develop policies and improve practice for refugee and asylum seeker tenants. Enhancing the quality of housing service and management, and providing accommodation and support better attuned to the needs of this tenant group requires proper resourcing and a comprehensive rather than an incremental approach which has been largely adopted to date.

In summary the main indicators for delivering good practice from the perception of the refugees and asylum seekers are as follows.

Despite the misgivings and criticisms of RSLs, overall the refugees and asylum seekers interviewed in this study recognise the benefits and appreciate the provision by RSLs. The majority appear satisfied with the physical accommodation, its maintenance and quality, especially where privacy is respected.

Good practice, in the perception of refugee and asylum seeker tenants, is the type of contact with landlords or support staff which provides either cultural affinity or a sense of belonging, for example, with own language documents. Aspects most valued were social factors including privacy, cultural and social activities and friendly staff. A possibly significant pointer is that negative experiences emanate from tenants in mainstream RSL properties.

The study reveals that the availability of RSL accommodation and the positive experiences of refugee and asylum seeker tenants are important factors in stimulating the well-documented process of secondary migration. Thus, anticipation of rising demand for RSL accommodation – accentuated by the statutory and nation policy trends – has very significant implications for RSLs in terms of the tenant mix of minority and specialist needs and the consequential letting practices, and management and support services they will need to offer.

The main concerns of respondents relate to access and allocation policies of RSLs which, in problematic cases, are perceived to be protracted, and to discriminate against the specific social and cultural needs.

In addition, this tenant group finds that the bureaucratic delays in dealing with complaints or maintenance needs are also a source of tension.

Refugees and asylum seekers have an array of distinctive yet diverse social and demographic characteristics which may increase their sense of vulnerability and heighten their sense of social exclusion and isolation. These aspects are not properly taken into account by RSLs, in the perception of the respondents. Attention is drawn to these very significant indicators of the ways in which RSLs need to develop sensitive and well-conceived policies and practices for management and service support which recognise these unique characteristics. The diversity of need is often overlooked within the process of bureaucratic labelling.

While the individual respondents provide vital insights into a number of aspects of housing access and services in the different localities, the role and capacity of community organisations, the RCOs, which represent these diverse groups, are equally significant.

That effective resettlement comes through a sense of autonomy and control over one's environment is a principle factor in the perception of well-being among the most satisfied refugee and asylum seeker tenants in RSLs. This has important implications for the way RSLs enable their tenants through participation, social and culturally sensitive support services and management practices which reflect the particular needs and experiences of this group.

Bad practice is, thankfully, not widespread, at least in the experience of the respondents. But there are already clear indicators of the need to substantially improve and sensitise existing practice, which our examination of RSLs in the next two chapters confirms. The extremely variable standards of response and the lack of specific provision tailored to the needs of particular refugee and asylum seeker groups, indicate a very limited appreciation of this diversity of need expressed by this group.

Appendix C: Research team and steering group membership

Research team

Martyn Pearl, Co-Director

Roger Zetter, Co-Director

Azim El-Hassan, Researcher

David Griffiths, Researcher

Sarah Birtles, Researcher

Steering group

David Ashmore, Chief Executive, Oxford Citizens Housing Association

Reena Mukherji, HACT

Chinta Kallie, formerly Oxford City Council

Areti Siani, formerly Refugee Council

Barbara Carlisle, The Housing Corporation

D

Appendix D: Organisations contacted for the study

Statutory bodies

Association of London Government (ALG)

Birmingham City Council

Home Office

London Boroughs of   Bexley

                          Brent

                          Hammersmith and Fulham

                          Hounslow

                          Newham

                          Tower Hamlets

                          Westminster

London Boroughs Grants Unit

Manchester City Council

Newham Community National Health Trust

The Housing Corporation

RSLs

Arawak/Walton Housing Association

Bethnal Green and Victoria Park Housing Association

Birmingham Friendship Housing Association

Bournville Village Trust

Bridge Housing Association

Ealing Family Housing Association

East Thames Housing Group

English Churches Housing Association

Family Housing Association

Focus Housing Association

Hexagon Housing Association

LABO

Mosscare Housing Association

Network Housing Association

North British Housing Association

Notting Hill Housing Trust

Oxford Citizens Housing Association

Peabody Housing Trust

Providence Row Housing Association

Refugee Housing Association

Refugee Housing Association (Handsworth)

South London Family Housing Association

Springboard Housing Association

St Mungo's Housing Association

Ujima Housing Association

Wandle Housing Association

Voluntary sector

Asylum Welcome

As-Shahada Housing Association

Camden Refugee Network

Children Society/Newham Family Homelessness Forum

Ethiopian Community in Britain

First African Housing Association

Islington Homelessness Forum

Karin Housing Association

King's Cross Homelessness Project

Manchester Refugee Support Network

Newham Refugee Support

Newham Somali Association

OMID

Praxis

Refugee Arrivals Project

Refugees in Oxford

Southwark Refugee Project

Tamil Refugee Housing Association

Others

Department of Sociology, University of East
London

Federation of Black Housing Organisations
(FBHO)

London Housing Federation

London Research Centre

Midlands Refugee Council

National Housing Federation

Red Cross Birmingham

Refugee Council

E

Appendix E: Survey questionnaire

The questionnaire below is one of three forms sent to local authorities, RSLs and voluntary organisations. Each form was tailored specifically towards one of these organisational types, the content below relating to RSLs. The questionnaire contained in this appendix is accurate in its content, but the format of the forms sent out differed to that below.

Asylum seekers, refugees and housing management in Registered Social Landlords

Please fill in the following section using CAPITAL LETTERS.

Full name of organisation _____

Address _____

_____

_____   Postcode _____

Contact name _____   Telephone _____

Job title _____

Fax _____   E-mail _____

Please answer the following questions by circling all the options that are appropriate, and giving details where necessary.

Please continue on a separate sheet if necessary.

1. What area does your organisation operate in? eg London, nationally.

_____

2. What is the total number of your housing stock?

Owned: No of units _____   Total capacity _____

Managed: No of units _____   Total capacity _____

3. Is your organisation registered as

1. Charity   2. Limited Company   3. Industrial and Provident Society

4. Housing association (fully registered with Housing Corporation)

5. Other please specify 5a _____

4. Is your organisation generalist or specialist? Please circle number as appropriate

1. Generalist   2. Specialist – Refugee and asylum seekers

3. Other. Please specify 4a _____

5. Does your organisation consider refugees and asylum seekers to represent a significant/special housing need in your area?

1. Yes.   2. No.

Please give a brief explanation _____

5a _____

_____

_____

_____

_____

_____

_____

6. Do you have specific policies regarding the housing of refugees and asylum seekers?

1. Yes – please give details at 6a   2. No – please go to 7

6a _____

7. Do you currently accept applications/nominations for housing refugees and asylum seekers from: Please circle numbers as appropriate and give examples.

1. Local authorities. Please give example. 1a

2. National bodies. Please give example. 2a _____

3. Voluntary agencies. Please give example. 3a _____

4. Refugee community organisations. Please give example. 4a _____

5. Self-referral asylum seekers. Please give example. 5a _____

6. Self-referral refugees. Please give example. 6a _____

7. Other. Please specify. 7a. _____

8. None of the above

8. How many refugees and asylum seekers have you housed in each of the last five years? Please state in terms of number of tenancies and total number of bedspaces

	1997	1996	1995	1994	1993
Tenancies	1___	3___	5___	7___	9___
Bedspaces	2___	4___	6___	8___	10___

9. Does your RSL work with any of the following agencies to provide housing or related services for refugees and asylum seekers?

1. Local authorities. Please give example. 1a _____

2. Community organisations. Please give example. 2a _____

3. Refugee community organisations. Please give example. 3a _____

4. Voluntary organisations. Please give example. 4a _____

5. National bodies. Please give example. 5a _____

6. Other RSLs. Please give example. 6a _____

7. Multi-agency groups. Please give details. 7a _____

8. Others. Please give example. 8a _____

9. None of the above

10. Has your organisation provided any training for staff in dealing with refugees and asylum seekers?

1. Yes – please give details at 10a   2. No – please go to 11

10 a _____

Please continue on a separate sheet if necessary

11. Are refugees and asylum seekers involved in management of stock (eg through community organisations, tenants associations) as policy advisers?

1. Yes – please give details at 11a   2. No – please go to 12

11a _____

_____

_____

_____

_____

_____

12. Please give examples of any successes your organisation has had in providing housing and related services.

_____

_____

_____

_____

_____

_____

_____

_____

Appendix F:
Refugee questionnaire

Refugees' and asylum seekers' experiences and responses to RSL housing.

This research is being carried out by Oxford Brookes University and is part of a wider survey of Registered Social Landlord (Housing Association) provision for refugees and asylum seekers.

For further information contact:

Roger Zetter and Martyn Pearl
School of Planning
Oxford Brookes University
Gipsy Lane
Headington
Oxford OX3 OBP (Tel 01865 483925)

This questionnaire is in two parts. The first part asks you questions which require short answers. The second part asks you questions where your own views can be discussed with the interviewer in more detail.

All information given on this form will be treated in strict confidence.

Part One

| To begin with, can you tell me about your background? |

1. Where are you from? (Bosnia = 1 Somalia = 2 Zaire = 3 etc)

_____

2. When did you arrive in the United Kingdom?

_____ (months from date of interview)

3. Can you tell me when you applied for asylum?

_____ (months from date of interview)

4. What status do you have at the moment?

1 = asylum seeker 2 = appeal outstanding 3 = Exceptional Leave to Remain 4 =full refugee status 5 =

5. What was your situation when you arrived in England?

1 = accompanied 2 = unaccompanied

6. If you were accompanied when you arrived where are these people now?

1 = living with respondent 2 = living elsewhere

7. Do you have a family who hope to join you?

1 = yes 2 = no

8. How many people will join you?

9. Before coming to your present address where did you live in the UK?

10. What type of accommodation was this?

1 = hostel 2 = homeless unit 3 = detention centre 4 = other housing association

5 =

11. Why did you leave this accommodation?

1 = short-stay 2 = problems with accommodation 3 = to join family members

4 =

12. When did you first come to _____ ? (months from date of interview _____)

13. Why did you come to _____ ?

1 = relatives and friends 2 = work 3 = accommodation 4 = support agencies 5 = release from detention 6 = bail provision

7 = educational opportunities 8 =

Can we now talk about your present situation?

14. What is your situation at the moment?

1 = full-time work 2 = part-time work 3 = temp work 4 = on benefits 5 = studying 6 = social services 7 = other support

15. When did you move in to your present accommodation?

_____ (months from date of interview)

16. What type of accommodation do you have?

1 = house 2 = flat 3 = hostel 4 = room 5 =

17. Can you tell me about your living arrangements?

1 = living alone 2 = sharing with family 3 = sharing with friends 4 =

18. Who pays the cost of accommodation?

1 = housing benefit 2 = self 3 = social services 4=

19. Is the accommodation

1 = furnished 2 = part-furnished 3 = unfurnished?

20. Have you received a copy of your tenancy agreement in your own language?

1 = yes 2 = no

> *Can you tell me about how you found your accommodation?*

21. Who helped you in finding your present accommodation?
1 = Refugee Arrivals Project   2 = community group   3 = Citizens Advice Group
4 = city/borough council   5 = friends/relatives   6 =

22. Did you have any problems in obtaining your current accommodation?
1 = yes   2 = no (if no, go to 24)

23. Can you tell me about these problems?
1 = lack of available places   2 = withdrawal of benefits   3 = changed family circumstances   4 = difficulty in obtaining an interview   5 = lack of information   6 =

> *Can we now move on to talk about your current accommodation in more detail?*

24. Do you know who to contact if you have any problems with your accommodation?
1 = yes   2 = no

25. Have you had, or are you currently having, any problems with your accommodation?
1 = yes   2 = no (if no, go to 28)

26. What kind of problems were they?
1 = repairs/maintenance   2 = overcrowding   3 = noise levels   4 = damp/heating
5 = harassment   6 = legal problems with tenancy   7 =

27. If you have had any problems how satisfied were you with the help you received?
1 = very helpful   2 = quite helpful   3 = helpful   4 = unhelpful   5 = very unhelpful

28. Have you ever made a complaint about the services you receive in your accommodation?
1 = yes   2 = no (if no, go to 31)

29. How did you make this complaint?
1 = on own   2 = with help   3 = in writing   4 = informal discussion   5 =

30. How did your landlord respond to your complaint?
1 = very helpful   2 = quite helpful   3 = helpful   4 = unhelpful   5 = very unhelpful

31. What are the best features of the services you receive?
1 = speed   2 =

> *Can you tell me if your landlord provides anything for you in addition to accommodation?*

32. Does your landlord provide any additional services?
1 = yes   2 = no (if no, go to 35)

33. What type of services are these?
1 = counselling   2 = interpretors   3 = welfare advice   4=

34. How satisfied are you with these services?
1 = very satisfied   2 = quite satisfied   3 = satisfied   4 = unsatisfied   5 = very unsatisfied

35. What additional services would you most like to see provided by your landlord?
1 = interpretors   2 = welfare advice   3 = counselling   4 = social/cultural events

> *I'd like to discuss with you if you feel included in the running of your accommodation.*

36. Do you know of any management committees or regular meetings?

I = yes 2 = no

37. Have you participated in these arrangements?

I = yes 2 = no (If yes, go to 39)

38. Can you tell me why you didn't participate?

I = not applicable 2 = unfriendly management 3 = lack of information 4 = language difficulties 5 = cultural differences
6 = gender differences 7 =

39. If you have participated, how successful was this?

I = very successful 2 = fairly successful 3 = successful 4 = unsuccessful 5 = very unsuccessful

40. How would you like your housing association to work in future?

I = encourage more participation 2 = more regular consultation 3 = more information
4 = to provide own-language materials 5 = to encourage same-sex representation 6 =

> *To complete this first section can you please answer some general questions about your current accommodation and what your future plans are?*

41. What do you think of the cost of your accommodation?

I = okay 2 = too high

42. Would you say that there are too many people living with you?

I = yes 2 = no

43. Is where you live good for work, social facilities and other services?

I = good 2 = average 3 = poor

44. Is where you live good for keeping in touch with friends and relatives?

I = good 2 = average 3 = poor

> *Looking to the future, can you tell me about your plans?*

45. If you had the opportunity to change your accommodation would you move?

I = yes 2= no (if no, go to Part Two)

46. If yes, what are your main reasons for wanting to move?

I = employment 2 = to be near family 3 = improve housing 4 = avoid harassment 5=

47. Where would you like to go?

I = other area in city 2 = other city 3 = London 4=

48. What is your preferred type of future accommodation?

I = owner-occupation 2 = council housing 3 = private rented 4 = other housing association 5 =

Part Two

> *Would you please discuss some issues in more detail with me?*

(The following are given as examples of the issues which may arise from the questionnaire.)

1. **What are the main advantages and disadvantages of your current accommodation?**

2. **Can you discuss your feelings about your current housing, eg levels of satisfaction, feelings of security and 'being at home'?**

3. **How important is the place you live in (location/housing) to you and how you would like to be housed in the future?**

4. **Do you feel that you have enough 'say' in the decisions that are made about your life, particularly in relation to housing?**

5. **What were the main problems you faced in finding your current accommodation?**

6. **What services would you most like to have provided by your landlord?**

7. **Are there any issues not raised in this questionnaire that you would like to discuss?**